D1349258

4 1 0260109 5

DIANA HENRY

SIMPLE

effortless food, big flavours

MITCHELL BEAZLEY

An Hachette UK Company
www.hachette.co.uk

First published in Great Britain in 2016
by Mitchell Beazley, a division of
Octopus Publishing Group Ltd
Carmelite House
50 Victoria Embankment
London EC4Y 0DZ
www.octopusbooks.co.uk

To Lucy, with love and thanks

ISBN 978 1 84533 897 8

A CIP catalogue record for this book is available
from the British Library.

Printed and bound in China

10 9 8 7 6 5 4 3 2 1

Publisher: Denise Bates
Art Director: Jonathan Christie
Photographer: Laura Edwards
Design and Art Direction: Miranda Harvey
Editor: Lucy Bannell
Home Economist and Food Stylist: Joss Herd
Assistant Home Economist: Rachel Wood
Senior Production Manager: Katherine Hockley

contents

introduction

In 2004 I wrote a book called *Cook Simple*, full of the kind of dishes I began to make when my first child was born. He cried constantly, so I was always carrying him and had no hands free. The more elaborate cooking I'd enjoyed before his arrival went out the window. In fact I ate takeaway pizzas for quite a few weeks after his birth, often through tears as I wondered how I would ever manage to cook again. Gradually, I started to make dishes that were just stuck in the oven. I didn't mind if they took a long time to cook, only about whether they took a long time to prepare. I couldn't do stir-fries – too much chopping – and rarely made risottos. It has meant a lot to me that people cite *Cook Simple* as a cookbook that really helped them. It's not because it is a book of quick food, but a book of *low-effort* food. Non-cooks and unsure cooks use it as much as people who feel totally at home in the kitchen.

Now the baby that forced me to change my cooking style is 17. I still – certainly during the week – like to cook food which doesn't take much hands-on time, and still bung a lot of dishes in the oven. But my life has changed; I can now manage risottos midweek, also fish or meat cooked on a griddle and served with a relish, or cooked in a frying pan in which a simple sauce is made. There are a few things – dals and other pulse dishes – which can simmer away on the hob while I do something else. So I felt it was time for a follow up to *Cook Simple*, time to offer a new collection of simple dishes that use a wider range of techniques.

I still think in 'blocks' when I wonder what to make for supper every day: fillets of fish – salmon or cod – or whole small fish, chops, sausages, pasta, chicken thighs, or potatoes for baking. I'm sure most people approach the evening meal like this. We buy what we can pick up easily on the way home, often from a small supermarket, or a local butcher or fishmonger. But this range of blocks has expanded. Our eating has changed in the last decade. Now I consider grains – often whole grains – pulses and a lot more vegetables, too. They don't have to be 'sides' to meat or fish, and this shift is reflected in the book.

UNUSUAL INGREDIENTS

The range of uncommon foodstuffs we eat – miso, pomegranate molasses, specific varieties of chillies – has also grown in the last decade. I don't use these just for the hell of it, but because I think they make eating more interesting, or are part of a cuisine I like. Most unusual items are now available online (and supermarkets have a vast array), but I've given alternatives where possible. There's a list of stockists at the back of the book, too. The matter of unfamiliar ingredients divides people: I get as many letters telling me they love discovering something new as I do from people complaining that they can't get pomegranate molasses at the corner shop.

HOW MANY PEOPLE DO THE RECIPES SERVE?

This was one of the hardest things to decide when writing the recipes. People have different appetites and I think we all, generally, eat less than we used to. My partner will always eat two chicken thighs, for example, but my kids only ever have one. So think who you are serving and what their appetites are like. When it comes to grain, salad and vegetable recipes, the question is even more difficult, as now we eat vegetable dishes as a main course. I've given as much guidance as I could. As a general rule, when it comes to vegetable dishes that serve six as a side dish, the recipe will serve four as a main meal.

COOKING EQUIPMENT

I never read those pages where writers lay out what you should have in your kitchen. For years – even after I started writing about food – I had the worst-equipped kitchen: not enough saucepans; one frying pan; a limited range of knives… But, apart from basics, there are a few things that will make cooking from this book easier. I often use a shallow broad cast-iron casserole with a lid that is 30cm (12in) in diameter. It's the most useful dish in my kitchen, and many of the recipes were tested in it so the cooking times are right for this size and dimension of dish. It's brilliant for bung-it-in-the-oven dishes as it allows chicken and vegetables to lie in a single layer and roast, rather than sweat as they would if they were piled on top of each other.

Roasting tins of various sizes are useful. If I say a leg of lamb or a chicken has to fit 'snugly' into a tin it's because the juices (especially when there's honey in a marinade) will burn if the space around the meat is too great. A gratin dish is important and a pudding or pie dish, too. I also have a food processor and wouldn't be without it. Electric beaters – you don't need a food mixer – are good for batters and whipping cream and are not expensive. It seems a small thing, but for grating ginger and garlic – and they appear a lot in this book – I use a Cuisipro fine grater. They're not cheap but they save time and hassle and are the best on the market, in my opinion. Finally, a mortar and pestle. I realize that might seem a little old-fashioned, but there are a lot of dishes in this book which require a bit of bashing. I like texture and sometimes food processors chop things too finely, especially if your attention wavers for a moment. So, a shallow casserole, a pie dish, a few roasting tins, a gratin dish, a mortar and pestle, a good grater and – if you can – a food processor are good to have.

There are two types of dish in *Simple*. Most are dishes you can cook midweek for your family, or for you and your partner; some are for weekend meals – Friday or Saturday night supper or Sunday lunch – to serve to friends (these are still simple, but take a bit more effort). There's no one who can't cook. You don't need many skills to feed yourself, your friends and family well. If you can shove a tray of red peppers into the oven, or cook pasta until al dente, you can make great food. What we mostly lack are ideas. That's what I tried to give in *Cook Simple* and, again, here. You don't have to be a chef. I'm not. You just need some inspiration to help you turn the ordinary – the building blocks of meals – into something special.

EGGS

egg & salmon donburi

DONBURI ARE JAPANESE dishes, simple concoctions served on a bowl
of rice. I've stolen this particular donburi from the Japanese restaurant
Nobu and adapted it. At the restaurant they serve it on sushi rice, but
you can use basmati, or not bother with the rice at all. It sounds quite
Puritan, but is really rich and satisfying; very quick to make, too.
I sometimes have pickled ginger and a dab of wasabi with it.

SERVES 2

100g (3½oz) brown or white basmati rice

150g (5½oz) salmon fillet, skinned

2 tsp extra virgin olive oil

2 tbsp very finely chopped onion

3 large eggs, lightly beaten

1 tbsp sake or dry sherry

1–2 tbsp light soy sauce

2–3 tbsp finely chopped avocado tossed with
   a little lemon juice

sesame seeds, black or white

1 sheet of toasted nori (optional)

Cook the rice in boiling water while you make the rest of the dish. With brown rice, just cook it
until tender (about 25 minutes). If you're cooking white rice, add just enough water to cover by
about 2.5cm (1in). Bring to the boil and, when the rice looks 'pitted' on the surface, reduce the
heat to its lowest, cover and leave to cook for 10–12 minutes, then fork it through.

To cook the salmon, put about 5cm (2in) of water in a pan and, when it's at a gentle simmer, add
the fish. Cover and poach over a very low heat for about two minutes. You want it raw in the
middle but cooked round the outside (though cook it right through if you prefer). Keep it warm.

Heat the olive oil in a small frying pan and gently sauté the onion until it is soft but not
coloured. Mix the eggs with the sake or sherry, add to the pan and cook very gently, stirring,
until you have a creamy mixture like soft scrambled eggs. Flake the warm fish and mix it with
the soy sauce.

Divide the rice between two bowls. Top each with half the eggs, fish, avocado and sesame seeds,
then crumble on the nori, if using. Add keta if you're going for luxury. Serve immediately.

persian-inspired eggs with dates & chilli

I LOVE THE IRANIAN FOOD SHOP, Persepolis, in south London. The first time I visited, I ate this fabulous dish in the café there, cooked by the owner, Sally Butcher. I have changed the recipe a bit – added some greens and onion – to make it into a more substantial lunch (Sally serves it with flatbread for breakfast). It sounds like a strange combination, I know, but it's addictive.

SERVES 1

½ tbsp olive oil
½ onion, finely sliced
½ tsp cumin seeds
¼ tsp chilli flakes
handful of baby spinach leaves
2 large eggs, lightly beaten
salt and pepper
2 soft dates (such as Medjool), pitted and roughly chopped
1 tbsp roughly chopped coriander leaves
Greek yogurt and flatbread, to serve (optional)

Heat the olive oil in a small frying pan and add the onion. Cook over a medium heat until it is golden and soft. Add the cumin and chilli and cook for another 30 seconds or so, then add the spinach. Keep turning the leaves over in the heat so they wilt and the moisture that comes out of them evaporates, then reduce the heat and add the eggs, seasoning and dates.

Cook quite gently, just as you would if you were making creamy scrambled eggs: the mixture should be soft set. Finally scatter on the coriander. Serve immediately, with a little yogurt on the side (if you've made quite a spicy plateful you'll need it) and flatbread, if you want.

menemen

I HAD ONLY EVER MADE menemen with baked eggs (the recipe is in my book *Food from Plenty*) until a holiday in Turkey a few years back when, every day, I had this version. I could honestly have eaten it for breakfast, lunch and dinner. Never have scrambled eggs tasted so good. Be careful to ensure that the vegetable mixture isn't too wet when you add the eggs.

SERVES 3–4

For the menemen
1 large leek
2 tbsp olive oil
1 red pepper, deseeded and finely chopped
1 green pepper, deseeded and finely chopped
salt and pepper
2 garlic cloves, crushed
pinch of chilli flakes, or ½ tsp cayenne pepper
4 tomatoes, deseeded and chopped
5 large eggs, lightly beaten

To serve (all optional)
warm flatbread
chopped dill, coriander or parsley leaves
crumbled feta cheese
natural yogurt

Remove the coarse outer leaves of the leek and trim the top – you need to get rid of the more tatty looking leaves – and the base. Slit the leek along its length and hold it under running water, fanning out the leaves and washing it well to get rid of any trapped soil. Chop it.

Heat the olive oil in a large frying pan. Add the leek, peppers and seasoning and cook over a medium heat – reduce the heat if they start to colour too much – until almost completely soft. Add the garlic and chilli or cayenne and cook for a minute, then add the tomatoes (to deseed tomatoes, quarter them, then just scoop or cut out the seeds from the surrounding flesh). Cook until they are soft, too, and their moisture has mostly evaporated (you might need to increase the heat to do this). It's important that the mixture isn't too wet, or the eggs won't scramble well.

Season the eggs, add them to the pan and cook over a very gentle heat, stirring all the time, until just set. Serve immediately with flatbread and any of the other accompaniments.

eggs with peppers & 'nduja

'NDUJA IS AN INGREDIENT that will become mainstream before too long. It's an intensely spicy pork paste from Calabria. You can get it in Italian delis and some online supermarkets now stock it, too.

SERVES 4
5 tbsp olive oil
1 large onion, finely chopped
3 red peppers, deseeded and sliced
salt and pepper
400g (14oz) cooked potatoes (unpeeled if waxy, peeled if floury), cut into chunks
85g (3oz) 'nduja
2 tbsp extra virgin olive oil
4 large eggs

Heat 3 tbsp of the regular olive oil in a large frying or sauté pan (preferably one you can serve from) and add the onion, peppers and seasoning. Cook until the vegetables are soft – about 25 minutes – keeping an eye on them and stirring every so often.

Meanwhile, heat the remaining 2 tbsp of regular olive oil in another frying pan and sauté the potatoes until they're golden and crusty all over. Season well.

Add the potatoes to the onion and peppers, toss together and add the 'nduja. Stir to break up the 'nduja and mix it well with the vegetables.

Heat the extra virgin olive oil in the pan you used for the potatoes and fry the eggs until the yolks have just set. Put the eggs on top of the 'nduja mixture and serve.

huevos rotos

SPANISH 'BROKEN EGGS'. Spicy, cheap, calls for a cold beer.
Perfect midweek food, in other words.

SERVES 2

6 tbsp extra virgin olive oil

1 large onion, very finely sliced

400g (14oz) waxy potatoes, peeled or unpeeled, sliced

salt and pepper

2 garlic cloves, crushed

2½ tsp smoked paprika

¼ tsp chilli flakes

2–4 eggs, depending on appetite

Heat the olive oil in a large non-stick frying pan over a medium heat and add the onion and potatoes. Fry for about 12 minutes, or until the potatoes are soft right through and everything is golden. Season, add the garlic and spices and cook for another four minutes.

Break the eggs one by one into the pan. You need to do this from a height – at least 30cm (12in) – so that the eggs crash into the mix. Season with salt and pepper and let them cook for a minute or so without stirring. You can scoop up some oil from the edge of the pan (tip the pan so you can do this) and spoon it over the eggs to help them set. Pierce the eggs – they are *rotos*, after all – so the yolks are just starting to run before serving.

sure as eggs

EGGS ARE A MIRACLE of natural architecture: delicate, lovely to hold and somehow complete in themselves. They've been enjoying a bit of a renaissance lately, partly due to the modern popularity of breakfast and brunch as a social occasion, but also because we find them so comforting. They're packed with protein, are perfect for vegetarians and those cutting down their meat intake, and have been given a clean bill of health, too. We now know that the dietary cholesterol in eggs doesn't have a significant effect on blood cholesterol. You can go to work on an egg and come home on one, too.

Time was when we couldn't think much beyond boiled and scrambled. Now I rustle up egg dishes from Japan, Iran and Turkey… and not just when there's nothing but eggs in the house. These are dishes I love. This chapter isn't about constructing risky soufflés, or sweating over glorious but demanding unguents such as hollandaise, it's about getting lunch or supper on the table quickly and easily, but with a bit of pizzazz.

Eggs need to be cooked with care, though. The biggest mistake we make with them is to apply too fierce a heat. Hot is fine if you're frying an egg and want a frilly edge, but most of the time it just makes eggs rubbery. Scrambled eggs, in particular, need to be cooked low and slow (adding a knob of butter at the end helps to stop them cooking). A panful of creamy, just-set scrambled eggs is one of the most luxurious things you can eat. Make the Japanese dish on page 10 and you'll see just how rich they can be. You shouldn't cook boiled eggs fiercely either, just at a vigorous simmer, otherwise the shells will crack. When poaching, use really fresh eggs – that stops the whites splaying – and very gently simmering water. Crack your egg into a cup, then carefully slide it into the pan. (I find that poaching in a frying pan works best.)

I care about the quality of the food I eat, and about its provenance, but I also try to be realistic about what people can afford. When it comes to flavour, though, there are some foods about which I cannot compromise: pork, butter and eggs are the three I would prefer not to eat at all if I couldn't get the best, as I know I will be disappointed with them. For years I bought free-range bog-standard eggs. Now I buy eggs from specific breeds – mostly Burford Browns and Cotswold Legbars (you can find them in the supermarket, you don't have to go to a farm shop) – because they taste so much better. If eggs are going to be the star of your lunch or supper, I think that the extra expense is more than justified (and compared to other foods, the extra is not *that* much). There's a bowl of pale blue Cotswold Legbar eggs on my kitchen counter right now. They aren't just beautiful, they also have limitless potential.

greens with chilli, olive oil, eggs, feta & seeds

MUCH QUICKER TO MAKE than it first appears. Fry the eggs rather than poaching, if it's easier (it always is for me).

SERVES 2

100g (3½oz) kale, coarse stalks removed, leaves torn

3 tbsp extra virgin olive oil, plus a little more to serve

125g (4½oz) spinach leaves, coarse stalks removed, roughly chopped

2 small garlic cloves, finely sliced

¼ tsp chilli flakes

salt and pepper

2 tbsp roughly chopped parsley or coriander leaves

squeeze of lemon juice

2 large eggs

2 slices of sourdough bread

25g (scant 1oz) feta cheese, crumbled

2 tsp pumpkin seeds, or any other seeds you prefer

Put the kale into a pot of boiling water and blanch it for five minutes. Drain really well, then squeeze out the water with your fists.

Heat 2 tbsp of the extra virgin olive oil in a frying pan and add the kale and spinach. Cook over a medium-high heat until the kale is heated through, the spinach has wilted and the water that comes out of the spinach has evaporated; this is *very* important. Add the remaining oil and the garlic and chilli. Sauté gently until the garlic is pale gold and everything is hot. Add the seasoning, herbs and a squeeze of lemon juice, the mixture should be warm and glossy. Cover to keep warm.

Quickly poach the eggs (see page 19) and toast the bread. Drizzle with a little olive oil. Pile the greens on to the toast, top each serving with an egg, sprinkle on the feta cheese and seeds and serve immediately.

leek & feta omelette
with sumac

WE SHOULD TAKE MORE EFFORT with omelettes. They tend to be made when there are only eggs in the house and cooked over too high a heat, giving a rubbery result. Think about the filling: cook it separately and let your imagination go. Try leek with goat's cheese and chopped black olives; or apple, leek and smoked Cheddar. These instructions are for one large omelette to serve two, but you can cook two smaller omelettes instead, if you prefer.

SERVES 2

1 large leek

½ tbsp olive oil

salt and pepper

1 garlic clove, crushed

10–15g (¼–½oz) unsalted butter

4 large eggs, lightly beaten

75g (2¾oz) feta cheese, crumbled

good pinch of sumac (optional)

Remove the coarse outer leaves of the leek and trim the tops – you need to get rid of the more tatty looking leaves – and the base. Slit along its length and hold it under running water, fanning out the leaves and washing it well to get rid of any trapped soil. Cut into 3–4cm (1¼–1½in) lengths.

Heat the oil in a non-stick frying pan, add the leek and seasoning and cook over a medium heat until completely soft (but not coloured; reduce the heat if it starts to brown). The mixture should be quite dry, so if it's at all wet increase the heat to drive off excess moisture. Add the garlic and cook for another couple of minutes. Check the seasoning, then scrape into a bowl.

Melt the butter in the same pan over a medium-low heat. Season the eggs, then add them to the pan. Using a wooden spoon, push the bits that are getting firm into the middle and swish the uncooked eggs around until they set as well. The bottom should be just firm but the top still a little runny.

Spoon the leeks and scatter the feta on half of the omelette, then, using a palette knife, fold the other half on top. Sprinkle the sumac over, if using (it just adds a tart citrus note) and serve.

parsi-style scrambled eggs

WHEN I'M DYING FOR A CURRY, I sometimes make this for supper: it sates that craving for a fraction of the price. The addition of a bit of cream makes it luxurious, too. Eat with warm naan bread.

SERVES 2

15g (½oz) unsalted butter

½ small onion, finely chopped

½–1 red chilli, depending on how hot you like it, deseeded and finely chopped

1 garlic clove, finely chopped

2 plum tomatoes, deseeded and finely chopped

4 large eggs, lightly beaten

2 tbsp double cream (optional)

salt and pepper

2 tbsp finely chopped coriander leaves

Melt the butter in a non-stick frying pan over a medium heat. Add the onion and cook, stirring from time to time, until soft but not coloured. Add the chilli and garlic and cook for a further two minutes, then add the tomatoes and cook until they have softened. Increase the heat to drive off excess moisture from the tomatoes, or the eggs won't scramble well.

Add the eggs, cream, if using, seasoning and half the coriander, then cook over a medium-low heat, stirring the eggs with a wooden spoon, until they form soft curds. Go slowly and gently. Sprinkle on the rest of the coriander and serve immediately.

SALADS

griddled courgettes, burrata & fregola

FREGOLA IS A SARDINIAN PASTA, about the size and shape of hailstones. If you can't find it, you could use Israeli couscous – that's the chunky type – as it looks quite similar. You can also use mozzarella if you can't find burrata.

SERVES 6 as a side dish, 4 as a main course

6 large or 12 medium courgettes

4 tbsp olive oil

salt and pepper

200g (7oz) fregola

2 tbsp extra virgin olive oil, plus more to serve

200g tub of burrata cheese

40g (1½oz) pecorino cheese, shaved, plus more to serve

leaves from 1 big bunch of basil, plus more to serve

juice of 1 large lemon

Cut the courgettes into rounds on the diagonal, about 4mm (¼in) thick. Heat some of the regular olive oil in a large frying pan and cook the courgettes, in batches, until golden on each side and tender. With each batch you need to start on a high heat to get a good colour, then reduce the heat so the slices can cook through. Season as you go and use more oil as you need it. Transfer each batch of cooked courgettes to a dish.

Cook the fregola in boiling salted water for 15 minutes, or according to the packet instructions, then drain, shake off the excess water and put into a mixing bowl. Toss with the extra virgin olive oil and seasoning.

Tear the burrata cheese into chunks. Layer up the various ingredients – courgettes, burrata cheese, pecorino cheese, basil, fregola, lemon juice and more extra virgin olive oil – in a broad shallow serving bowl. Finish with basil, shavings of pecorino cheese and a final drizzle of extra virgin olive oil. Serve while still warm, or at room temperature.

cucumber, radishes & cherries with rose petals

THIS IS LIKE EATING A GARDEN. It's fresh and pretty with both crisp and soft textures. Mint or dill work just as well as tarragon.

SERVES 4

For the dressing
¾ tbsp white wine vinegar
smidgen of Dijon mustard
salt and pepper
6 tbsp olive oil
1½ tbsp double cream
chopped leaves from 7 sprigs of tarragon
1½ tsp caster sugar, or to taste

For the salad
1 small cucumber, or ½ large cucumber
  (about 250g/9oz)
200g (7oz) cherries
150g (5½oz) radishes (ideally both crimson
  and purple), trimmed and shaved or
  very finely sliced
40g (1½oz) pea shoots
handful of unsprayed rose petals, torn
  if large, left whole if small

To make the dressing, mix the vinegar, mustard and seasoning in a small bowl. Whisk in the oil and cream with 1½ tbsp of water. Add the tarragon and sugar. Mix and taste; you may want to adjust the seasoning. The consistency should be about that of single cream.

Peel the cucumber in stripes, so some of the skin is left on (it just looks nice). Halve lengthways and scoop out the seeds with a teaspoon. Discard them. Cut into slices about 3mm (⅛in) thick, or cut the cucumber into ribbons using a vegetable peeler.

Pit the cherries; I like to tear them in half to do this, rather than cut them. Put the cucumber, radishes and pea shoots into a broad shallow serving bowl and toss together with three-quarters of the dressing. Add the cherries and drizzle the remaining dressing over the top (as the cherry juice 'bleeds' over the salad, it's best to add them last). Scatter on the rose petals and serve.

cumin-coriander roast carrots with pomegranates & avocado

AN IDEA SHAMELESSLY STOLEN from New York-based chef April Bloomfield and slightly mucked about with. Roasted carrots and avocados are surprisingly good together. This makes a very grand platter to open a meal, or serve it on the side with roast chicken, or with another vegetable dish.

SERVES 6 as a starter, or 8 as a side dish

For the salad
30 young carrots, ideally slim
4 tbsp extra virgin olive oil
2 tsp cumin seeds
1½ tsp coriander seeds, crushed
1 tsp chilli flakes
salt and pepper
3 ripe avocados
25g (scant 1oz) walnut pieces, toasted (page 112)
100g (3½oz) watercress, coarse stalks removed
leaves from a small bunch of coriander

250g (9oz) Greek yogurt
1 garlic clove, crushed
seeds from ½ pomegranate

For the dressing
3 tsp pomegranate molasses
1 garlic clove, crushed
¼ tsp Dijon mustard
6 tbsp extra virgin olive oil
¼ tsp honey
squeeze of lemon juice

Preheat the oven to 200°C/400°F/gas mark 6. Trim the carrots at the tops but leave a bit of green tuft on. If you can't find slim carrots, halve or quarter large ones. Don't peel them, just wash well. Put in a roasting tin in which they can lie in a single layer. Add the olive oil, spices and seasoning. Turn the carrots over in this to ensure they are all well coated. Roast in the oven for about 30 minutes; they will become tender and shrink slightly. Be careful not to overcook them.

To make the dressing, just whisk everything together with a fork. Halve and pit the avocados, cut into slices, then carefully peel each slice. Put everything except the yogurt, garlic and pomegranates into a broad shallow bowl (or on to a platter) and gently toss in three-quarters of the dressing. Mix the yogurt with the garlic and dot spoonfuls of this among the vegetables, then scatter with the pomegranate seeds. Spoon on the rest of the dressing and serve.

tomatoes, soft herbs & feta with pomegranate

A SALAD I FIRST ATE IN ISTANBUL. The pomegranate flavour here is in the dressing, not in the seeds. You can make this salad even when pomegranates are not in season.

SERVES 6

For the dressing
1 tbsp white balsamic vinegar
1 tbsp pomegranate molasses
1 tsp honey
1 garlic clove, crushed
salt and pepper
3 tbsp extra virgin olive oil
lemon juice, to taste (optional)

For the salad
handful of flat leaf parsley leaves
500g (1lb 2oz) well-flavoured tomatoes (a mixture of colours is lovely if you can find them)
handful of dill fronds, roughly torn
2 small shallots, very finely sliced
150g (5½oz) barrel-aged feta cheese, drained of brine
4 tbsp pomegranate seeds (optional)

Put the vinegar, pomegranate molasses, honey, garlic and seasoning into a small bowl, then whisk in the olive oil. Taste for seasoning. Add a squeeze of lemon juice if you think it needs it.

Set aside some of the best-shaped parsley leaves and roughly chop the rest.

Slice the tomatoes, or halve them if they are small. Put into a serving dish and add the dill, chopped parsley, shallots and dressing. Crumble the feta cheese on top.

Toss very gently – you don't want to break up the feta cheese too much – then sprinkle on the pomegranate seeds, if using, and the whole parsley leaves and serve immediately.

root, shiitake & noodle salad with miso dressing

I LOVE BROWN RICE NOODLES. They're so earthy. If you want to extend this, add shredded sugar snaps (sliced lengthways, no need to cook), edamame, finely sliced radishes, even avocado. This dressing is great; it's worth making double or even triple the amount here and keeping it in the fridge… it will soon disappear.

SERVES 8 as a side dish, 4 as a main course

For the dressing
4 tsp white miso
3 tsp honey
2 tsp rice vinegar
1 red chilli, deseeded and finely sliced
3 tbsp groundnut oil
2 tsp soy sauce
2 tsp sesame oil
3 tbsp sweet pickled ginger,
   finely chopped

For the salad
100g (3½oz) mooli (daikon), cut into matchsticks
2 medium carrots, peeled
2 tbsp groundnut oil
400g (14oz) shiitake mushrooms, sliced
salt and pepper
230g (8oz) brown rice noodles
120g (4¼oz) baby spinach leaves
6 spring onions, trimmed and chopped at an angle
2 tsp white sesame seeds
2 tsp black sesame seeds (or more white sesame)

To make the dressing, whisk the miso, honey and vinegar together, then whisk in everything else. It will seem quite strong, but you're going to add it to noodles so it needs to be assertive. Drop the mooli matchsticks into iced water to crisp up. Cut the carrots into matchsticks, or shave them: trim the tops, lay on the work top and peel them, working away from you. When one side is flat, turn it and do the other side. You'll have some left; keep it for something else.

Heat the oil in a frying pan and briskly cook the mushrooms over a high heat. Season well.

Put the noodles into boiling water and soak for eight minutes. Drain and rinse in cold water. Shake excess water out, then throw into a serving bowl with half the dressing; I find it easiest to toss this with my hands. Drain the mooli; add to the bowl with the carrots, mushrooms, spinach and spring onions. Sprinkle with the remaining dressing and the sesame seeds and serve.

cool greens with hot asian dressing

You can put whatever you like in this... as long as it's green: kale, Chinese leaf, small courgettes, raw young peas, broad beans, whatever. You can reduce the range, too, you don't have to use all the herbs. Take care with the dressing, it needs a good sweet-sour-salty-hot balance so taste as you go and adjust it before tossing with the vegetables.

SERVES 6–8

For the dressing
1½ generous tbsp caster sugar, or to taste
juice of 2–3 limes (they vary a lot in juiciness), or to taste
1½ tbsp fish sauce, or to taste
2cm (¾in) root ginger, peeled and finely grated
2 red chillies, deseeded and very finely chopped
1 garlic clove, crushed
¾ tbsp sunflower or groundnut oil

For the greens
75g (2¾oz) edamame beans
1 avocado
juice of 1 lime
salt and pepper
100g (3½oz) sugar snap peas, sliced lengthways
75g (2¾oz) mooli (daikon), cut into matchsticks, or radishes, finely sliced
½ ridge cucumber, peeled and chopped
3 spring onions, trimmed and chopped
50g (1¾oz) baby spinach, or mixed green leaves
leaves from 1 bunch each of coriander, basil and mint
sesame seeds, ideally mixed black and white

Using a fork, whisk the sugar with 1½ tbsp of boiling water to help the sugar dissolve. Add the lime juice (keep a little back as limes vary in juiciness). Add the fish sauce, ginger, chillies and garlic, then whisk in the oil. Taste for sweet-salty balance. You might want more lime juice, or even more sugar or fish sauce: use your taste buds. Remember this is a strong dressing.

Boil the edamame beans for three minutes, drain and allow to cool. Halve the avocado, pit it, then slice. Peel each slice, squeeze lime juice over and season. Put all the vegetables, leaves and herbs into a broad shallow bowl. Toss with the dressing, top with the sesame seeds and serve.

food52 team salad

FOOD52 IS ONE OF THE BEST food websites. Based in New York, it's classy and well designed and has great recipes. I visit the site pretty much every day, so it was a big thrill to meet the team behind it when I was last in the States. This is the salad they rustled up for lunch (I've tweaked it only a little), served with various cheeses and breads. I had never felt well-disposed towards kohlrabi, but this changed my mind. If you can't find watermelon radishes (though Ocado now supply them), just use more kohlrabi or beetroots.

SERVES 4–6 as a side dish
120g (4¼oz) kohlrabi
225g (8oz) mixed beetroots (ideally regular, golden and candy stripe)
135g (4¾oz) watermelon radish
1 eating apple
2 tbsp lemon juice
1 tbsp white balsamic vinegar
1 tsp honey
salt and pepper
4 tbsp extra virgin olive oil (a fruity rather than a bitter, grassy type)
2 tbsp lightly toasted hazelnuts, halved (see page 281)

Peel the kohlrabi, beetroots and watermelon radish. Shave them all on a mandolin, or cut very, very finely with a sharp knife. Do the same with the apple, leaving it whole and working from each side towards the core: that way you will get good circles, but without the core (just eat the flesh round that, cook's treat).

Make a dressing by mixing the lemon juice, vinegar, honey and seasoning. Whisk in the oil.

Spread the vegetables and apple out in a broad shallow bowl, dressing them as you go, then scatter the nuts on top. The crimson in the beetroots will start to stain everything else, so it's better to layer the vegetables than it is to toss them. Serve immediately.

salad of chorizo, avocado & peppers with sherry dressing

To make a more gutsy dish, balance a fried egg for each person on top before you scatter on the breadcrumbs.

Serves 4 as a main course

For the salad
3 red peppers, halved and deseeded
olive oil
salt and pepper
2 ripe avocados
lemon juice
55g (2oz) open-crumbed loaf (sourdough or
   ciabatta), torn into small pieces
extra virgin olive oil
finely grated zest of ½ unwaxed lemon

225g (8oz) chorizo
400g can of chickpeas, drained and rinsed
75g (2¾oz) rocket, baby spinach, lamb's lettuce
   or watercress, coarse stalks removed
generous handful of coriander leaves

For the dressing
1 tbsp sherry vinegar
5 tbsp extra virgin olive oil
2 tsp medium sherry
1 tsp honey

Preheat the oven to 190°C/375°F/gas mark 5. Drizzle the peppers with the regular olive oil, season and roast for about 35 minutes, or until completely soft. Leave to cool a little.

Make the dressing by whisking everything together and seasoning well. Halve the avocados, pit them and cut the flesh into slices lengthways. Carefully peel each slice. Squeeze a little lemon juice over the avocados to keep them from discolouring and season.

Slice the peppers (I don't remove the skins). Fry the torn-up bread in a little extra virgin olive oil over a medium heat, tossing so it doesn't burn but becomes golden and crunchy. In the final stages of cooking, add the lemon zest and season. Remove the chorizo skin and cut into rounds. Put 1 tbsp of regular olive oil in a frying pan and quickly sauté it on both sides until golden.

Gently toss everything, except the bread, with the dressing. Scatter over the bread and serve.

south-east asian fruit salad with chilli & tamarind

BASED ON A SALAD called *rojak* or *rujak* (the word means 'mixture' or 'wild mix'). There are many variations, but some are almost entirely based on fruit. You could add matchsticks of raw jicama to this if you can find some, but I rarely can. The dressing usually contains shrimp paste, which I hate, so I've used fish sauce instead; use shrimp paste if you don't mind it. You can add herbs – coriander, basil or mint leaves, or a mixture – as well, even though that's not authentic.

SERVES 6 as a side dish

For the salad
1 Granny Smith apple
juice of 1 lime
2 mangoes, slightly under-ripe
350g (12oz) prepared pineapple (about
    1 small fruit), cut into chunks
½ ridge cucumber, peeled, cut into chunks
200g (7oz) cherry tomatoes, quartered
½ tbsp sesame seeds
15g (½oz) roasted peanuts, roughly chopped

For the dressing
1 tbsp tamarind paste
¾ tbsp fish sauce
juice of ½ lime
1 tbsp palm sugar, or soft light brown sugar
½ tsp sambal oelek (Indonesian chilli paste), or to taste

Halve, core and cut the apple into matchsticks, immediately dropping them into a serving dish with the lime juice (this stops it discolouring). Peel the mangoes, then remove the 'cheeks' (the fat bits on each side). Cut into cubes, then remove the rest of the flesh as neatly as possible and cut that into cubes, too. Toss into the bowl with the pineapple, cucumber and tomatoes.

For the dressing, stir the tamarind, fish sauce and lime juice with the sugar until it dissolves. Add the sambal oelek and 2 tbsp of water. It will taste strong, but it works with the fruit.

Toss the dressing with the salad in the bowl and scatter with the sesame seeds and peanuts.

smoked trout, eggs & keta with sour cream dressing

A BEAUTIFUL-LOOKING DISH that takes very little effort. Using keta (salmon caviar) does make it pricey, but I love those little bursts of saltiness against the potatoes and eggs. It's not an everyday ingredient, but it makes a lovely weekend lunch or brunch, and is just as good at Christmas as in the spring.

SERVES 6 as a main course

For the salad
500g (1lb 2oz) baby potatoes
2 tbsp white wine vinegar
100ml (3½fl oz) fruity extra virgin olive oil
salt and pepper
6 eggs
375g (13oz) smoked trout
60g (2¼oz) baby leaves (whatever you can find)
fronds from about 12 sprigs of dill, torn
10g (¼oz) chives, halved
50g jar of keta (salmon roe)

For the dressing
120g (4½fl oz) sour cream
1 tbsp double cream
2 tsp Dijon mustard
juice of ½ small lemon

Boil or steam the potatoes until just tender. Slice them and gently mix in a bowl with the vinegar, two-thirds of the olive oil and some seasoning. Leave to cool. Make the dressing by mixing everything together. Cook the eggs for seven minutes, run cold water over them to cool them a bit, then peel and halve.

Flake the trout and gently combine in a bowl with the rest of the olive oil, seasoning, the potatoes (with their dressing), leaves and herbs. Arrange on a platter – or in in a broad shallow bowl – and add the eggs. Spoon the creamy dressing over the top (or serve it under the salad) and dot with little spoonfuls of the keta. Serve immediately.

melon, blueberry & feta salad with ginger & mint

YES, I DO ADORE salads made with fruit, but melons can be musky and muted and blueberries – if you get good fruit – have a little tartness, too. Then there's the salty feta cheese to cut the sweetness. You can leave out the blueberries here, if they seem a fruit too far.

SERVES 6 as a side dish, 4 as a main course

For the salad
175g (6oz) watermelon flesh, neatly sliced (seeds flicked out)
235g (8½oz) Ogen melon flesh (about ½ melon), neatly sliced
235g (8½oz) Galia melon flesh (about ½ melon), neatly sliced
½ cucumber, peeled
100g (3½oz) blueberries
20g (¾oz) mint leaves
125g (4½oz) barrel-aged feta cheese, crumbled or chopped
1 tbsp roughly chopped pistachio nuts

For the dressing
juice of 2½ limes
3½ tbsp vinegar from a jar of pickled ginger
1 tbsp runny honey
3½ tbsp extra virgin olive oil
1 tsp peeled and finely grated root ginger
salt and pepper

Put the mixed melon flesh into a broad, shallow serving dish. Slice the cucumber very thinly and add it to the melon with the blueberries.

Mix everything for the dressing together.

Tear any large mint leaves in half, leaving small leaves whole and add to the salad with most of the dressing. Sprinkle on the feta cheese and nuts, drizzle on the rest of the dressing and serve.

warm salad of squid, bacon, beans & tarragon

IF YOU BUY CLEANED SQUID – and that's easy to get now – this is very quick to put together. It makes a good starter, light lunch or supper. Add warm sliced waxy potatoes if you want to make it more substantial.

SERVES 3–4

For the dressing
2 tbsp lemon juice, plus more for the squid
2 tbsp extra virgin olive oil
6 tbsp double cream
leaves from 6 sprigs of tarragon, chopped
salt and pepper

For the salad
600g (1lb 5oz) squid (preferably small), cleaned
½ tbsp olive oil, plus more for the squid
2 shallots, finely sliced
200g (7oz) bacon lardons
225g (8oz) French beans, topped but not tailed

For the dressing, mix the lemon juice, extra virgin olive oil, cream, tarragon and 2 tbsp of water in a small bowl. Season.

Cut the wings from the squid and put them aside with the tentacles. Cut the bodies down one side so they open out. If your squid are big, halve the body lengthways. Wash and dry the squid well on kitchen paper, then put in a bowl with enough regular olive oil to moisten them.

Gently cook the shallots in the ½ tbsp of regular olive oil until they have lost their rawness but aren't soft. Put into a broad shallow serving bowl. Add the bacon to the same pan and cook over a high heat until golden all over and cooked through. Add to the shallots. Cook the beans in boiling water until al dente. Drain and run cold water over them. Pat dry and toss into the bowl.

Heat a frying pan until very hot. Season the squid and cook it quickly on both sides in batches; you want to get a lovely golden colour. Squeeze over lemon juice as soon as it's ready. Toss it with the other ingredients in the serving bowl. Spoon on the dressing and check the seasoning.

burrata with citrus, fennel & olives

Quite a special dish – burrata isn't cheap – so this is more of a treat recipe, though good mozzarella can be used instead of burrata.

Serves 6

For the dressing
6 tbsp orange juice, or to taste
1 tbsp lemon juice
2 tsp runny honey, or to taste
6 tbsp extra virgin olive oil (fruity rather than grassy), plus more for the burrata
salt and pepper

For the salad
2 oranges
1 pink grapefruit
1 white grapefruit
1 large fennel bulb
about 30 top-quality black olives, pitted
2 x 200g tubs of burrata cheese

Make the dressing by putting all the ingredients for it in a cup and whisking together with a fork. Taste for seasoning and balance.

Cut a slice from the bottom and top of each citrus fruit so they have a flat base on which to sit. Using a very sharp knife, cut the rind and the pith off, removing them in strips from top to bottom and working your way round the fruit. Now slice the fruits, removing any seeds you see.

Quarter the fennel and remove the coarse outer leaves. Trim off any fronds and keep them for later. Remove the core from each quarter, but don't allow the quarters to fall apart. Cut very finely – wafer-thin slices are best – using a mandolin if you have one, or a very sharp knife.

Carefully toss the fennel, citrus and olives together, or arrange them on plates, with the dressing. Drain the burrata cheeses (be careful; they are fragile), then tear into pieces and put on top of the salad, or serve them whole. Drizzle with extra virgin olive oil and grind on black pepper. Serve immediately.

no-hassle starters

Starters are my favourite bit of any meal. They're small and light and they set the tone. I find it difficult not to offer a starter, even if I have friends round midweek, so I've amassed a repertoire of dishes that take hardly any effort. Here's some of them.

QUICK-CURED SALMON & BUTTERMILK
This is stolen from the wonderful Stephen Harris at The Sportsman in Kent. Take 500g (1lb 2oz) good skinless salmon fillet, sprinkle with 200g (7oz) sea salt flakes mixed with 150g (5½oz) soft brown sugar. Cover and chill for 24 hours. Rinse and slice as you would smoked salmon. Mix 2½ tbsp icing sugar, the juice of 2 lemons and 115ml (3¾fl oz) vodka. Marinate the salmon in this for 10 minutes. Mix 200ml (7fl oz) buttermilk, ½ tsp Dijon mustard, 1 tbsp extra virgin olive oil, salt and a pinch of sugar. Serve with the fish, shaved radishes and dill.

DEVILLED EGGS
The first thing I cooked in domestic science, these have had a renaissance. Boil 4 large eggs for 7 minutes. Leave to cool. Peel, halve, scoop out the yolks and mash with 3 tbsp good mayo, a knob of soft butter, a good shake of Tabasco, 1 tsp chopped parsley, 1 tsp mustard powder and ½ tsp white wine vinegar. Season. Put this back in the whites, sprinkle with cayenne and serve with all the sass of a Southern hostess.

ROASTED SPICED CHICKPEAS
I love crisps but not with drinks (no matter how 'posh'). For this good, easy alternative, preheat the oven to 190°C/375°F/gas mark 5. Drain, rinse and dry a 400g can of chickpeas (or even 2, people eat a lot once they start these). Toss them with 1 tbsp olive oil, ½ tbsp ground cumin, ½ tbsp chilli powder, salt and pepper. Spread out on a baking sheet and bake for 30 minutes, shaking around every so often.

A LITTLE SCANDI FEAST
You don't even need to cook for this (except for the eggs). Serve cured herrings, a jar of keta, a bowl of sour cream with chopped dill, smoked fish, cured ham, sweet-savoury pickled cucumber, cooked beetroots and hard-boiled eggs. Offer rye bread or knäckebröd (you can get such good crispbreads these days), great butter and chilled vodka. Good for brunch as well as for a starter.

CROSTINI WITH LARDO & HONEY
Seems just too easy? People will love it. Lightly toast slices of ciabatta; put furls of lardo on top; drizzle with good honey. That's it.

PEACHES WITH BURRATA
A perfect summer starter. Slice ripe peaches, carefully tear burrata and put on a platter. Add basil, season, squeeze over lemon juice and drizzle with your favourite olive oil. Tomatoes and Parma ham are optional additions.

SMOKED FISH BUTERBRODY

A Russian treat. Mash 300g (10½oz) good smoked trout or mackerel with 1½ tbsp creamed horseradish, 75g (2¾oz) soft butter, 1 tbsp thick cream, the yolks of 2 hard-boiled eggs, the juice of ½ lemon, salt and pepper. Spread on squares of pumpernickel or rye (crusts off and toasted if you're using rye).

PEAS & MELTED BUTTER

Yes, seriously. When they're young and have just come into season, boil them in their pods and serve in a bowl with a pot of melted butter.

MINIMAL MEZZE

This doesn't have to be a massive spread. Offer hot Moroccan or Middle Eastern pickles, really good taramasalata (not the dyed stuff), feta that you've marinated in extra virgin olive oil with some garlic, thyme and chilli flakes, roast peppers (you can buy them in jars), olives and flatbread. If you can manage something the day before, make labneh: put Greek yogurt into a new J-cloth, form it into a bag, squeeze it, then put it in a sieve set over a bowl. Let the whey drip off in the fridge overnight. Drizzle it with good extra virgin olive oil and sprinkle with za'atar, dukkah or sumac.

PEA & 'NDUJA TOASTS

'Nduja is the chorizo *de nos jours*, a spicy Calabrian pork paste that is totally addictive and is catching on everywhere. Serve it on little toasted croûtes (ciabatta or slices of baguette). Purée 100g (3½oz) cooked peas with ½ crushed garlic clove, ½ tbsp lemon juice, a few mint leaves, 2 tbsp extra virgin olive oil, ½ tbsp double cream and seasoning. Spoon on to the toasts, then place chunks of 'njuda on top.

TOAST

carrot houmous, roast tomatoes & harissa yogurt

THIS MAKES MORE HOUMOUS than you need for a meal, but it's a real pain to use only half a can of anything. Keep the rest of the houmous in the fridge, where it will last for about three days. The tomatoes are really useful to have in the fridge, too. I often cook double quantities of them; they're great on toast with labneh (see page 51), eggs or mashed avocado.

SERVES 4

For the roast tomatoes
8 plum tomatoes
2 tbsp olive oil
½ tbsp balsamic vinegar
2 tsp harissa
salt and pepper
1 tsp soft light brown sugar

For the houmous and yogurt
250g (9oz) carrots, peeled and chopped
400g can of chickpeas, drained and rinsed
200ml (7fl oz) extra virgin olive oil
3½ tbsp tahini
juice of 1½ lemons
½ tsp cayenne pepper
1 tsp ground cumin
250g (9oz) Greek yogurt
1 tbsp harissa
4 slices of sourdough bread, or bread of your choice

Preheat the oven to 190°C/375°F/gas mark 5. Halve the tomatoes lengthways and put in a small roasting tin or ovenproof dish; they need to fit fairly snugly in a single layer. Mix together the regular olive oil, vinegar, harissa and some seasoning and pour this over the tomatoes. Turn the tomatoes over to coat them in oil, then rearrange them cut sides up. Sprinkle over the sugar and roast for 40–45 minutes, or until shrunken and sweet.

Cook the carrots in boiling water until they're tender. Drain, reserving some cooking liquid, then whizz in a food processor with everything else except the yogurt, harissa and bread. Add some of the cooking water if you need it, to make the purée a little thinner. Scrape into a bowl.

Stir the yogurt to loosen it, put it into a bowl and spoon on the harissa. Toast the bread and serve it with the houmous, tomatoes and yogurt.

mumbai toastie

OH, MY. MY FRIEND ROOPA GULATI told me about these – they're sold as street food in Mumbai – and I was a bit sceptical about cheese with spices, but these toasties now make a regular appearance in my house. They're perfect for those nights when you're craving Indian food, but don't want to splash out on a takeaway. A great telly-watching supper. You'll want a cold beer.

SERVES 1

For the fresh chutney
½ green chilli, deseeded and chopped
handful of coriander leaves
leaves from 8 sprigs of mint, torn
1 garlic clove, crushed
sea salt flakes
½ tsp caster sugar
juice of ½ lemon

For the sandwich
2 slices of white bread
50g (1¾oz) Cheddar, Lancashire or Wensleydale
    cheese, grated or very finely sliced
1 tomato, sliced
¼ small red onion, very finely sliced
pinch of ground cumin
pinch of ground coriander
pinch of ground ginger
pinch of ground cinnamon
unsalted butter
¼ tbsp vegetable oil (optional)

Put everything for the chutney, except the lemon juice, in a mortar and pound it with the pestle. You can just chop everything together instead, but the chutney is better if it has had a good pounding. Add the lemon juice.

Spread the chutney over both slices of bread. Lay the cheese, tomato and onion on one of them and sprinkle with the spices. Top with the other piece of bread.

If you have a toastie maker, use it, buttering the outside of the sandwich as usual, or melt a knob of butter and the oil in a frying pan and cook it over a medium heat for about three minutes on each side, weighing it down (I use a flat saucepan lid with a heavy can on top). Be careful not to burn the sandwich, and adjust the heat accordingly. The cheese should melt. Serve immediately.

toast with crab & coriander-chilli mayo

A TREAT FOR TWO. Good for lunch on a Saturday.

SERVES 2

35g (1¼oz) mayonnaise
½ tbsp double cream
finely grated zest of ½ lime, plus a couple of squeezes of lime juice
1 small red chilli
2 tbsp finely chopped coriander leaves
2 slices of sourdough bread
salt and pepper
100g (3½oz) white crab meat, picked over
unsalted butter
2 small handfuls of watercress, coarse stalks removed

Mix the mayonnaise with the cream and add the lime zest and a squeeze of juice. Halve the chilli, remove the seeds and cut into fine shreds. Stir this and the coriander into the mayonnaise and mix well.

Toast the sourdough, season the crab meat and add another squeeze of lime juice. Butter the toasts, put the crab on top, then add a good dollop of the mayo. (You can stir the mayonnaise into the crab and eat it that way, too, but I prefer to come across some plain, unadorned crab every now and again here.) Serve with watercress.

cider rarebit

ADDING AN EGG is not to everyone's taste (or everyone's idea of
what a rarebit should be), but I like it. It turns a snack into a very
good supper. And that's not the only twiddle you can make. Try this
with sautéed slices of apple or pear (lay these on the bread before
adding the cheese mixture). I've even been known to add bacon…
A green salad and a glass of cider are perfect on the side.

SERVES 2

25g (scant 1oz) unsalted butter
25g (scant 1oz) plain flour
125ml (4fl oz) dry cider
100g (3½oz) grated mature Cheddar cheese
1 tsp English mustard (made mustard, not powder)
shake of Worcestershire sauce (optional)
2 slices of bread from a good white bloomer
pepper
1 egg, lightly beaten
½ tbsp apple brandy or Calvados

Preheat the grill: some can take quite a while to get hot enough.

Melt the butter in a saucepan and add the flour. Stir over a medium heat until they blend and
thicken to form a roux. Take the pan off the heat and pour in the cider, a little at a time, stirring
well after each addition and beating to make sure no lumps form. Put the pan back on the hob
and stir as you bring the mixture to the boil. You should end up with a smooth, thick sauce.
Reduce the heat to low and add the cheese, mustard and Worcestershire sauce, if using.

Toast the bread.

Stir the sauce to help the cheese melt completely, then remove from the heat, season with
pepper and add the egg and brandy, stirring well. Divide between the two slices of toast –
I then put these in a flameproof gratin dish but that's just to save the grill pan – and grill
until bubbling and golden.

crunch time

TOAST IS ESSENTIALLY a private pleasure, not something we often serve to others (except at breakfast). It's also, for me, the go-to emotional food. If I'm unhappy, I think I deserve toast. When I feel tired and need a pick-me-up, I wait for a slice of sourdough to pop. When I had post-natal depression, toast with lots of butter was the only food that could over-ride my lack of appetite and break through the bleakness. That makes it special. I'm not alone in my ardour. Toast is a British love. Chewy, warm and slightly nutty, it's the mother of all comfort foods, a friend in good times and in bad.

Now that we take bread more seriously, we are beginning to think toast more important, too. As long as you use good bread and top it with something that has the healthy seal of approval (nut butter, crushed avocado, local honey), it's mandatory to show off your toast via Instagram and Twitter. When I met Apollonia Poilâne, whose family produce the world-famous Poilâne sourdough, she served me a feast of... toast, explaining that sourdough actually tastes best several days after baking, toasted, as this brings out its characteristic tang. A few years back, San Franciscans – as is their wont – went all hipster about toast. Critics touted the $3 slice of artisanal toast as proof that this food-obsessed city had become a parody of itself. But they were doing good things with it. Cafés developed 'toast bar' menus, and every time I visited a classy American food website someone had come up with a new twist on avo toast.

We Brits can claim a greater toast history than Californians, though. We've been putting interesting things on toast since the Middle Ages ('pokerounce', toast topped with hot honey, ginger and cinnamon, sounds particularly good, as does quince purée with flower water). Then there are 'savouries', specifically English treats of toast topped with anchovies, grated cheese or ham and served at the end of dinner, so beloved of the Victorians and Edwardians. Food historian Dr Annie Gray says we love toast because we have such a big bread culture in Britain. 'Toast is a sensible way of using the remains of the loaf from the day before: it's thrifty. The kind of bread we like here lasts quite well, too, unlike French baguette which is basically so hard the day after it's made, it's impossible to do anything with it.'

Now toast has become the basis for a decent meal again: a proper lunch, a nourishing supper. It's especially useful if you're on your own, or there's just two of you. There are no rules about preparing it, though you should use good bread. Cheap sliced bread made by the Chorleywood method will be pappy inside; you want a toasted exterior and a good fluffy interior. It's also best to stand your newly toasted slice up against something so it cools just slightly before adding your topping. This prevents sogginess. And you wouldn't want that.

toasted brioche with boozy mushrooms

A REAL JOY. If you don't want the sweetness of brioche here, use toasted sourdough bread instead. This can take a fried egg on top, too. The obvious thing might be to add garlic and parsley but, in fact, unadulterated mushroominess is what you want.

SERVES 2

10–15g (¼–½oz) dried wild mushrooms

1½ tbsp olive oil

250g (9oz) chestnut mushrooms, or mixed mushrooms, roughly chopped (you want quite big pieces)

75ml (2½fl oz) dry sherry or vermouth

salt and pepper

75ml (2½fl oz) double cream

2 slices of brioche loaf

Put the dried mushrooms in a small bowl and add enough boiling water to just cover them. Leave to sit for about 20 minutes.

Heat the oil in a frying pan and add the fresh mushrooms. You'll think it's a lot for two people, but mushrooms really shrink. Cook them briskly over a fairly high heat to get a good colour, you need to keep moving them around. When they're golden brown and the juices they give off have evaporated, add the dried mushrooms with their soaking liquid. Cook until the soaking liquid has almost disappeared, then add the alcohol and seasoning. Cook over a high heat until half the booze has disappeared, then add the cream.

Toast the brioche. Keep cooking the mushrooms until they are just coated in cream. Check for seasoning, then tip on to the toasts and serve.

spiced avocado with black beans, sour cream & cheese

AVOCADO TOAST has almost become a cliché – I've lost count of the ways I've seen it prepared – but it's also irresistible (and good for you). This makes a bit more of the avo-on-toast theme. Remember that the key to any avo toast is good seasoning.

SERVES 4

For the black beans
1 tbsp olive oil
½ onion, finely chopped
1 red pepper, deseeded and chopped
  into small squares
2 garlic cloves, crushed
½ tsp ground cumin
75ml (2½fl oz) chicken or vegetable stock
25ml (scant 1fl oz) orange juice
salt and pepper
400g can of black beans, drained and rinsed
juice of ½ lime

For the toasts
4 slices of sourdough bread
1 garlic clove
4 tbsp extra virgin olive oil
4 small, ripe avocados
juice of 1–2 limes (depending on how juicy they are)
2 red chillies, deseeded and finely sliced
4 spring onions, finely chopped
4 tbsp sour cream
2 tbsp roughly chopped coriander leaves
4 tbsp feta or Wensleydale cheese, crumbled

Make the beans first. Heat the regular olive oil in a saucepan over a medium heat and sauté the onion and pepper until the onion softens. Add the garlic and cumin and cook for another two minutes. Pour on the stock, orange juice and seasoning and cook over a low heat until the vegetables are tender. Add the beans, season, heat through and add the lime juice.

Toast the bread and rub it with the garlic. Drizzle with a little of the extra virgin olive oil, then scoop out the avocado flesh and spread it roughly on top. Season, drizzle with the rest of the extra virgin olive oil, squeeze on some lime juice and scatter with chillies and spring onions. Top with the black beans and serve with sour cream and coriander, sprinkling on the cheese.

warm eggs, roast tomatoes & watercress cream

I LOVE THE DIFFERENT temperatures here: warm toast and eggs; tomatoes at room temperature; cold watercress cream. When pushed – and when tomatoes are good – I make this with raw tomatoes. It's really important that the egg yolks are still just a bit soft in the centre and that you crush and eat the eggs while they're still warm.

SERVES 4

8 large eggs
100g (3½oz) mayonnaise
2 tbsp sour cream or crème fraîche
30g (1oz) watercress, coarse stalks removed, finely chopped
½ tsp Dijon mustard
squeeze of lemon juice
4 slices of sourdough bread
unsalted butter
salt and pepper
1 quantity of Roast tomatoes (see page 54), made without harissa

Boil the eggs for seven minutes; they should still be a little soft in the centre.

Meanwhile, make the watercress cream. Put the mayonnaise, cream, watercress, mustard and lemon juice into a small food processor and whizz. Or, if you don't have a small food processor, just finely chop the watercress and mix it with the other ingredients.

Toast the bread. Drain the eggs and plunge them into cold water. As soon as they are just cool enough to handle, peel them. Butter the toasts, crush the eggs on to them, season, top with the tomatoes and spoon on some of the watercress cream. Eat immediately.

mashed eggs with anchovy, shallots & parsley

MORE SOFT, WARM EGGS. Sometimes I leave this shallot topping raw. It's sharp and strong in flavour that way, and that's what you fancy from time to time. The cooked version – as given below – is more nuanced.

SERVES 2

2 large eggs
3 tbsp extra virgin olive oil
½ shallot, finely sliced
3 anchovies, finely chopped
½ tbsp finely chopped flat leaf parsley leaves
pepper
2 slices of sourdough bread
1 garlic clove

Boil the eggs for seven minutes; they should still be a little soft in the centre.

Meanwhile, heat 2 tbsp of the olive oil in a small frying pan and sauté the shallot and anchovies over a medium-low heat, just to take the raw edge off the shallots. The anchovies will break down a little. Add the parsley and season with pepper.

Toast the sourdough and rub each piece with the garlic. Drizzle the remaining 1 tbsp of olive oil over both slices.

Drain the eggs and plunge them into cold water. As soon as they are just cool enough to handle, peel them. Roughly break up each egg on a slice of sourdough – I do it directly on the toasts – then spoon the shallot and anchovy mixture over each serving.

salmon tartare
& avocado on rye

A FAVOURITE SPIN on the avo-on-toast theme. If you want to be
fancy, a dollop of sour cream and a spoonful of keta (salmon roe)
looks lovely and tastes gorgeous, too. Since I'm a bit of a Puritan,
I only allow that at the weekend…

SERVES 2

For the tartare
150g (5½oz) salmon fillet, skinned
1 small shallot, very finely chopped
1 tbsp finely chopped dill fronds
½ tbsp lemon juice
2 tbsp extra virgin olive oil (fruity rather
    than grassy)
salt and pepper

For the toasts
2 slices of rye bread
1 large, ripe avocado
lemon juice
avocado oil
2 crisp fresh radishes, cut into matchsticks

Cut the salmon into small cubes, about 5mm (¼in) square. Put this in a bowl with
everything else for the tartare. Mix and taste, seasoning well.

Toast the rye bread. Scoop out the flesh from the avocado and mash it roughly on the toasts.
Squeeze on some lemon juice, season and drizzle with avocado oil. Spoon some tartare on
top and sprinkle with the radishes.

goat's cheese & roast grape tartine

CHEESE ON TOAST, FRENCH STYLE. If you're roasting grapes for this, you might as well roast a larger amount. They are lovely in a salad with bitter leaves – such as radicchio – crumbled Gorgonzola cheese and toasted walnuts.

SERVES 2

150g (5½oz) seedless black grapes
1 tbsp olive oil
½ tbsp balsamic vinegar
2 slices of sourdough bread
125g (4½oz) spreadable goat's cheese
1½ tbsp extra virgin olive oil
pepper
10g (¼oz) walnuts, toasted (see page 112)
a little honey (optional)
dressed salad leaves, to serve

Preheat the oven to 200°C/400°F/gas mark 6.

Put the grapes on a baking sheet and drizzle with the regular olive oil and the vinegar. Bake for 15–20 minutes.

Lightly toast the sourdough, but don't let it turn too golden as you are going to grill it further. Spread the goat's cheese thickly on the toasts, then drizzle with the extra virgin olive oil and season with pepper. Put the grapes on top and grill for two minutes, or until the cheese is golden in patches. Sprinkle on the walnuts and drizzle with a little honey (if using). Serve immediately with some leaves on the side.

PULSES

cumin-roast aubergines, chickpeas, walnuts & dates

THIS IS SO EASY. Stick the veg in the oven, make the dressing, heat the chickpeas and voilà. It's great with couscous, but also makes a fabulous side dish for roast lamb or grilled mackerel.

SERVES 4

For the aubergines
3 aubergines, about 750g (1lb 10oz) in total
3 smallish onions
6 tbsp olive oil
3 tsp ground cumin
2 tsp Aleppo pepper
salt and pepper
400g can of chickpeas, drained and rinsed
good squeeze of lemon juice
10g (¼oz) coriander leaves, chopped
1½ tbsp date syrup

5 fat sticky dates, such as Medjool, pitted
  and chopped
15g (½oz) walnut pieces, toasted (see page 112)

For the dressing
50ml (2fl oz) tahini
50ml (2fl oz) extra virgin olive oil
1 fat garlic clove, crushed
4 tbsp Greek yogurt
juice of ½ lemon

Preheat the oven to 190°C/375°F/gas mark 5. Cut the aubergines horizontally into slices about 2cm (¾in) thick, then halve the larger slices. Halve the onions and cut into crescent-shaped wedges. Put the aubergines and onions into a roasting tin, drizzle with 5 tbsp of the regular olive oil and add the cumin, Aleppo pepper and some seasoning. Mix it all together and roast for 45 minutes, tossing everything around every so often. The aubergines will shrink a lot. For the dressing, put everything into a blender with 50ml (2fl oz) of water and blitz. It should be the consistency of pourable thick cream. Add more water if it is too thick, then check the seasoning.

When the aubergines are nearly cooked, heat the final 1 tbsp of regular olive oil in a frying pan and warm the chickpeas through. Season, add a squeeze of lemon juice and tip into a broad, shallow bowl. Stir the coriander into the aubergines and pile on top. Drizzle with the dressing, then with the date syrup. Scatter the dates and nuts on top and serve.

simple red lentil & pumpkin dal

Simple to whip up any time, as long as you have a bit of pumpkin lying around (though I've also used a mixture of carrots and parsnips when desperate and very good it was, too). Proper dals (Indian lentil stews) are finished with a 'tarka' – a last-minute seasoning of fried spices and, sometimes, curry leaves – but when I'm in a hurry I forego this.

Serves 6

3 tbsp rapeseed or sunflower oil

1 large onion, finely chopped

500g (1lb 2oz) sweet pumpkin or butternut squash, peeled, deseeded and cut into 2.5cm (1in) chunks (prepared weight)

150g (5½oz) tomatoes, chopped

3 garlic cloves, crushed

2 tsp chilli flakes

3cm (1¼in) root ginger, peeled and grated

2 tsp ground cumin

½ tsp ground turmeric

225g (8oz) red lentils

salt and pepper

3 tbsp chopped coriander leaves (optional)

Heat half the oil in a heavy-based saucepan and fry the onion until it is golden brown. Heat the rest of the oil in a frying pan and sauté the pumpkin until the pieces are golden all over.

Add the tomatoes to the onion and cook for another four minutes, then add the garlic and spices and cook for two minutes, stirring a little. Add the lentils and pumpkin to the onions and pour on 1 litre (1¾ pints) of water. Season (this needs plenty of salt) and bring to the boil. Reduce the heat and cook for 20 minutes, until the lentils have collapsed and the pumpkin is tender. The mixture should be thick.

Check the seasoning. Serve with the coriander sprinkled on top, if you like. Eat with rice or flatbread and offer yogurt on the side.

breton tuna & white bean gratin

A GREAT STORECUPBOARD RECIPE which is much more delicious than you might expect: rich and satisfying. You don't need any starch on the side, just a green vegetable or salad. Ideally, you want a 200g can of tuna but, as they can be hard to find, a 160g can will do.

SERVES 4

½ tbsp olive oil

1 onion, finely chopped

6 garlic cloves, finely sliced

2 x 400g cans of haricot beans

salt and pepper

2 tbsp double cream

2 tbsp milk

200g or 160g can of tuna in olive oil (see recipe introduction)

1 small dried red chilli, crumbled (optional)

40g (1½oz) grated Gruyère cheese

2 tbsp coarse white breadcrumbs

15g (½oz) unsalted butter

½ tbsp chopped parsley leaves

Preheat the oven to 180°C/350°F/gas mark 4.

Heat the olive oil in a frying pan and sauté the onion until soft but not coloured (about five minutes). Add the garlic and cook for another four minutes or so. Drain one of the cans of beans and add them to the pan, then add the other with its juices (the juices are good for texture). Season really well and place over a low heat so that the beans can meld with the onion.

Put the mixture into a food processor and blitz to a purée. Add the cream and milk and whizz again. Tip into a bowl and add the tuna along with the oil in which it's canned, the chilli, if using, and half the cheese. Stir together and taste for seasoning.

Scrape the mixture into a small gratin dish. Sprinkle the breadcrumbs and the rest of the cheese on top. Put little nuggets of butter all over the crumbs and bake for 20 minutes, sprinkling the parsley on five minutes before the end. The gratin should be golden and bubbling; if it isn't, cook it for five minutes longer.

Serve with a green vegetable, such as broccoli.

indian sweet potatoes with chickpeas & coconut

A WONDERFUL DISH FOR A CROWD. You just need yogurt, rice and chutney on the side. Use pumpkin instead of sweet potatoes, or replace some of the sweet potatoes with regular potatoes (waxy are best), if you prefer. You can get unsweetened coconut chips from health food shops (or see page 330), but leave them out if you can't find them.

SERVES 8

2 tbsp groundnut oil

2 large onions, roughly chopped

3 tsp ground cumin

2½ tsp ground coriander

1½ tsp ground turmeric

1 red chilli, deseeded and finely chopped
   (or leave some seeds in if you
   want more heat)

2.5cm (1in) root ginger, peeled and
   finely grated

3 garlic cloves, crushed

bunch of coriander, leaves and stalks separated

8 tomatoes, roughly chopped

3 sweet potatoes, peeled and cut into chunks

salt and pepper

3 x 160ml cans of coconut cream

400g can of chickpeas, drained and rinsed

400g (14oz) spinach, any coarse stalks removed

juice of ½–1 lime

handful of dried, unsweetened coconut chips
   (plain or toasted)

Heat the oil in a large saucepan over a medium heat and add the onions. Cook for 10 minutes, stirring occasionally, until soft and golden. Stir in the dried spices and cook for two minutes, then add the chilli, ginger, garlic, finely chopped coriander stalks and tomatoes. Cook for five minutes, stirring from time to time.

Add the sweet potatoes and 500ml (18fl oz) of water, season and bring to the boil. Reduce the heat to a simmer, cover and cook for 10–15 minutes. Add the coconut cream and chickpeas, then cook for 15–20 minutes, stirring often, until the sweet potato is cooked and the sauce thickened.

Stir in the spinach and allow it to wilt; it will only take a few minutes. Add the lime juice and taste for seasoning. Chop the coriander leaves and sprinkle them on with the coconut chips.

baked merguez with beans, eggs & feta

THIS IS AN EASY MEAL – and looks great – but you need to get the sauce right, adjusting its consistency around the sausages by cooking it a little longer if you need it to be thicker, or adding more water if you want it thinner. I can't be specific, as it depends on the size of pan you're using, so just adjust until you get it the way you like it. Your seasoning needs to be good, too. Be assertive.

SERVES 6 GENEROUSLY

1½ tbsp olive oil

12 merguez, or spicy lamb, sausages

1 large onion, finely chopped

3 garlic cloves, crushed

2 x 400g cans of cherry tomatoes

salt and pepper

¼ tbsp dried oregano

grated nutmeg (I use nearly ½ in this)

1 tbsp soft light brown sugar (the tomatoes need it)

extra virgin olive oil

2 x 400g cans of white beans (haricot or cannellini), drained and rinsed

400g can of butter beans, drained and rinsed

6 large eggs

cayenne pepper

50g (1¾oz) feta cheese, crumbled

Heat the regular olive oil in a large, broad pan (mine is 30cm/12in and cast iron). Quickly brown the sausages all over on a high heat to get a good colour, then set aside. Add the onion and cook over a medium heat until soft and pale gold, then add the garlic and cook for another minute. Pour in the canned tomatoes and season really well. Sprinkle in the oregano, nutmeg and sugar. Bring to the boil, reduce the heat, return the sausages to the pan plus a good slug of extra virgin olive oil (it really enriches the dish) and simmer gently for about 20 minutes.

Now add both types of beans and gently stir. Add more seasoning – beans need a lot – and perhaps a little water. You want a dish that is thick, with the beans coated in tomato sauce, but the liquid will reduce as you now should cook it for another 20 minutes, over low heat, stirring gently from time to time. If it isn't thick enough, cook for a little longer. Check the seasoning.

Break the eggs on top and allow them to cook until the whites are set (you can cover the pan to speed this up). Sprinkle a little cayenne on each egg, then add the feta. Serve immediately.

harissa roast carrots, white beans & dill

I LOVE TO LOOK at an ingredient in a different light. After years of regarding dill as the quintessential Scandinavian herb, it was a pleasing surprise to find it's used just as much in the Middle East, Turkey and Greece. The fresh piney-ness is gorgeous against the oily heat of harissa.

SERVES 6

For the carrots

750g (1lb 10oz) slim carrots, with green tops
1 lemon, very finely sliced (flick the seeds out),
    plus juice of ½
2 tbsp harissa
4 tbsp olive oil
2 tsp cumin seeds
2 garlic cloves, crushed
2 tsp honey
250g (9oz) Greek yogurt
2 tbsp extra virgin olive oil, plus more to serve
4 tbsp buttermilk, or whole milk

For the beans

2 tbsp olive oil
½ onion, roughly chopped
1 garlic clove, crushed
2 x 400g cans of haricot or cannellini beans,
    drained and rinsed
about 60ml (2fl oz) chicken or vegetable stock
salt and pepper
3–4 tbsp extra virgin olive oil
good squeeze of lemon juice
15g (½oz) dill fronds, plus 1 tbsp to serve

Preheat the oven to 200°C/400°F/gas mark 6. Trim the carrots, leaving green tufts. If the carrots are chunky, halve lengthways. Put into a roasting tin in a single layer (but without masses of room, or the juices burn). Add the lemon slices. Mix the harissa, regular olive oil, cumin, garlic, honey and lemon juice and toss with the carrots. Roast for 30–35 minutes, turning halfway, until tender. For the beans, heat the regular olive oil in a saucepan and gently cook the onion until soft but not coloured. Add the garlic, beans, stock and seasoning. Cook over a medium heat for two minutes. Stir in the extra virgin olive oil and lemon juice, then the dill. Taste for seasoning.

Mix the yogurt with the extra virgin olive oil, buttermilk or milk and seasoning. Put the beans into a dish with the carrots and lemon slices on top. Spoon a little yogurt over (serve the rest on the side), then scatter with the 1 tbsp of dill. Pour a little extra virgin olive oil on top and serve.

canned love

WE'RE ALL SUPPOSED TO eat fresh and seasonal these days, and cook from scratch. I'm always preaching it. But there is a shelf in my larder that I wholeheartedly love (it's my favourite shelf to organize). It is stacked with cans. And these are not standbys. Canned tomatoes are a total necessity and nobody thinks you shouldn't use them because Italians do it, too, right? But there's a very impressive supply of various canned beans and fish, too… and some of the packaging for them is so beautiful that I have to *make* myself use the contents rather than hoard them.

They're partly for emergencies because sometimes, despite my job, I forget to think about the evening meal and have to throw something together, but I like them, too. Purists may be horrified – and, weight for weight, canned beans are certainly more expensive than dried – but I use them an awful lot. No cans of cannellini beans? It's a crisis. No canned anchovies? How could I let that happen? Canned beans aren't always a good alternative to the dried variety, though. Dishes such as cassoulet – where the beans become deliciously imbued with fat, herbs and stock as they cook for hours – are better made with dried beans. Nevertheless, I don't often have time for that kind of cooking.

Creamy canned flageolets with garlic, cream and parsley are amazing alongside lamb chops: they're not Michelin star but they're satisfying, the kind of thing a chic-but-harassed French woman would make. Canned chickpea mash, the beans crushed with sautéed onions, loads of garlic, cumin, lemon juice and a good dollop of harissa, is fantastic with purple-sprouting broccoli (and I can't tell the difference between home-cooked and good canned chickpeas anyway).

A can of anchovies, chopped and gently heated in a pan with garlic, chilli and olive oil until they melt, then finished with parsley: that can go on my pasta any day, or my fish, or even lamb chops for that matter. Even Greek baked beans – a dish that is usually made really slowly – can be perfectly delicious when made with cans. You just need to take care not to cook the canned beans so much that they fall apart. Treat them gently.

Opening a can and quickly throwing a dish together gives me a real buzz. I'm getting a bit of help, but I still have the fun part to do: the seasoning, the tasting. It's the kind of cooking most of us do when we start out. I didn't learn about cooking by making lobster à l'américaine; I started by using sautéed onions, peppers and a can of haricots to make spicy beans.

Okay, I'm not suggesting you use canned potatoes (not even those from France), but you should feel proud of the get-it-on-the-table-quickly cooking that other cans make possible. It's about turning the ordinary into something special. So stock up with pride.

El *Velero*
CONSERVAS
ORTIZ

ANCHOAS en aceite de oliva

FILETS DE SARDINES
SANS PEAU

les *enfandines*
A LA
TOMATE

Connétable
DEPUIS 1853

VINTAGE 2002
CHOICEST FISH
IN PUREST OLIVE OIL

By Special Royal Permission
KING OSCAR BRAND
BRISLING
IN PUREST OLIVE OIL

DESDE 1891
CONSERVAS
ORTIZ
El *Velero*

BONITO DEL NORTE
EN ACEITE DE
OLIVA

thyme-baked mushrooms & borlotti with roast garlic crème fraîche

ROASTED MUSHROOMS offer a big dose of umami – they're deeply meaty and savoury – and you don't have to do much with them. Season, drizzle with olive oil and a little vinegar and bung them in the oven. The beans here mute their meatiness slightly, and add an earthy sweetness. If you don't want to go to the bother of roasting the garlic, just crush a small raw garlic clove and stir it into the crème fraîche instead.

SERVES 4 as a side dish

500g (1lb 2oz) portabellini or portobello mushrooms, carefully wiped clean
1 large onion, cut into wedges about 2cm (¾in) thick
6 tbsp olive oil
2 tbsp balsamic vinegar
8 sprigs of thyme

salt and pepper
1 small garlic bulb
1 tbsp extra virgin olive oil, plus more to serve
400g can of borlotti beans, drained and rinsed
juice of ½ lemon
150g (5½oz) crème fraîche

Preheat the oven to 200°C/400°F/gas mark 6. If you have larger portobello mushrooms, slice thickly. Put the mushrooms and onion in a roasting tin where they can lie in single layer. It looks a lot, but they shrink. Toss with 5 tbsp of the regular olive oil, the vinegar, thyme and seasoning. Cut the top off the garlic and seal the bulb into a foil parcel with a splash of water and the 1 tbsp of extra virgin olive oil. Set on a baking sheet. Roast the garlic and mushrooms for 45 minutes. Mushrooms throw out a lot of water, but it should evaporate; they should also be dark. When there are 10 minutes to go, heat the remaining 1 tbsp of regular olive oil in a frying pan and quickly sauté the beans. Season well. Add to the mushrooms while they finish cooking.

Toss the contents of the roasting tin. If they seem wet, set on a medium-high heat and boil most of the moisture off. Tip into a warm bowl. Add the lemon and drizzle with extra virgin olive oil. Squeeze the garlic out of its skins, mash, then stir into the crème fraîche. Serve alongside.

greek baked beans with dill, preserved lemon & feta

MUCH MORE THAN the sum of its parts. It's rich, but made from humble ingredients – olive oil and slow cooking does this – and the herbs, cheese and lemon make it special... even if preserved lemons are Moroccan, rather than Greek. Jars of cooked beans are much more expensive than canned, but they are luscious. If you want a cheaper option, use three 400g cans of cannellini or butter beans (or a mixture) instead of jarred beans.

SERVES 6 as a main course

2 tbsp extra virgin olive oil, plus more to serve
1 large onion, roughly chopped
2 medium carrots, peeled and finely chopped
2 celery sticks, finely chopped
3 garlic cloves, crushed
2 x 400g cans of cherry tomatoes in thick juice
salt and pepper
1–2 tsp soft light brown sugar

2 tsp dried oregano
1 bay leaf
2 x 625g jars of large cooked white beans
10g (¼oz) dill fronds, chopped
100g (3½oz) feta cheese, crumbled
1 preserved lemon (½ if home-made; 1 if bought), fleshy bits removed, rind cut into shreds

Preheat the oven to 180°C/350°F/gas mark 4. Heat the olive oil in a casserole and sauté the onion, carrots and celery until soft, but not coloured. Add the garlic and cook for another few minutes. Add the tomatoes and bring to the boil, pressing the tomatoes to crush them. Simmer for about 10 minutes. Season well and stir in the sugar, oregano, bay and beans.

Cover and bake for 30 minutes, then stir and return to the oven without a lid. Bake for another 30 minutes, checking once or twice, until the liquid has reduced and the mixture is thick. Stir in a glug of oil and the dill and check the seasoning. Serve sprinkled with the feta cheese and preserved lemon. A bowl of yogurt is lovely on the side.

roast cauliflower with pomegranates, green olives & chickpea purée

A SALAD OF POMEGRANATES, green olives and walnuts is common in Turkey and that's how this dish started off. If you don't want to make the chickpea purée then just toss drained chickpeas into the dish, or add cooked farro, spelt or wheat berries to make it into a big salad (you'll need more lemon, extra virgin olive oil and seasoning).

SERVES 4 as a main course, 6 as a side dish or mezze

For the cauliflower
florets from 1 large cauliflower
1 tsp cayenne pepper
1½ tsp cumin seeds
4 tbsp olive oil
salt and pepper
30g (1oz) walnuts, toasted (see page 112)
115g (4oz) green olives, pitted and chopped
leaves from a bunch of coriander, chopped
juice of ½–1 lemon, to taste

about 1 tbsp extra virgin olive oil
seeds from ½ pomegranate

For the chickpea purée
400g can of chickpeas, drained and rinsed
1 garlic clove, crushed
1½ tbsp tahini
1 tsp ground cumin
1 heaped tsp cayenne pepper
150ml (5fl oz) extra virgin olive oil
juice of 1 lemon, or to taste

Preheat the oven to 200°C/400°F/gas mark 6. Put the cauliflower into a roasting tin in which it can lie in a single layer. Add the cayenne and cumin, the regular olive oil and seasoning. Toss with your hands and roast for 30–35 minutes. Toss occasionally so the cauliflower gets golden all over. Meanwhile, make the purée. Purée the chickpeas in a food processor with the garlic, tahini, cumin and cayenne, then add the extra virgin olive oil in a steady stream. Add the lemon juice to taste. Season and add enough water to get the texture you want. Check the seasoning.

When the cauliflower is cooked, toss in the walnuts, olives, coriander and lemon juice. Drizzle with the extra virgin olive oil and scatter with pomegranate seeds. Serve with the purée. If this is to be a main course, couscous or bulgar wheat with chopped preserved lemons stirred into it makes a very good side dish.

lamb & bulgar pilaf with figs & preserved lemons

BULGAR PILAFS only take 20 minutes to cook. This recipe is good for using up leftover roast lamb. To avoid the expense of fresh figs (though they look and taste gorgeous), you can use 50g (1¾oz) of moist dried figs, chopped, soaked in just-boiled water for 30 minutes, then drained.

SERVES 4

3 tbsp olive oil

8 fresh figs, stalks snipped off, halved

500g (1lb 2oz) lamb leg steak, cut into chunks (or see recipe introduction)

1 large onion, roughly chopped

¼ tsp chilli flakes

½ tsp ground allspice

3 tsp ground cumin

1 garlic clove, crushed

175g (6oz) bulgar wheat

350ml (12fl oz) lamb stock

salt and pepper

25g (scant 1oz) raisins

½ x 400g can of chickpeas, drained and rinsed

35g (1¼oz) walnut pieces, toasted (see page 112)

2 tbsp chopped flat leaf parsley and coriander leaves

2 preserved lemons (1 if home-made; 2 if bought), fleshy bits removed, rind cut into shreds

Heat 1½ tbsp of the olive oil in a sauté pan and, when it's really hot, quickly cook the figs, cut sides down first, until they are tender and golden on the cut sides. Remove and set aside.

Add the rest of the oil and brown the lamb in two batches over a high heat until it has a good colour all over, taking each batch out as it is browned. Add the onion and cook for about eight minutes, first on a high heat to get a decent colour, then on a low heat to help it soften. Stir in the chilli, allspice, cumin and garlic and sauté for another two minutes. Add the bulgar wheat and stir to coat in the oily juices. Pour in the stock and add seasoning, tip in the raisins and return the lamb. Bring to the boil, then immediately reduce the heat to low. Cover the pan and cook for 15 minutes, until the liquid has been absorbed and the bulgar is tender. Season.

Gently fork in the chickpeas. Cover again and leave for another 10 minutes off the heat to allow the bulgar to fluff up. Gently fork through the nuts, herbs and preserved lemons, then transfer to a heated bowl and put the figs on top. Serve with Greek yogurt on the side.

PASTA
& GRAINS

pappardelle with cavolo nero, chilli & hazelnuts

ONE OF MY FAVOURITE DISHES is pasta tossed with garlic, chilli, parsley, olive oil and orange zest. I've simply added cabbage and nuts here to make it a bit healthier (and quite a lot more delicious).

SERVES 4

400g (14oz) pappardelle
salt and pepper
700g (1lb 9oz) cavolo nero
5 tbsp extra virgin olive oil, plus more to serve
3 garlic cloves, finely sliced
2 red chillies, deseeded and chopped, or about ½ tsp chilli flakes
finely grated zest of ½ large orange
40g (1½oz) hazelnuts, halved and toasted (see page 281)
25g (scant 1oz) flat leaf parsley leaves, roughly chopped
finely grated Parmesan cheese, to serve

Put the pasta in a large pan of boiling salted water and cook until al dente, about 15 minutes, or a minute or so less than suggested on the packet instructions. Meanwhile, remove the tough ribs from the cavolo nero (discard them) and wash the leaves. Plunge into boiling water and cook for seven minutes. Drain well. Squeeze the excess water from the cabbage with your hands and chop it roughly.

When the pasta has about four minutes left to cook, heat the oil and gently sauté the garlic and chillies until the garlic is pale gold. Add the zest and cabbage, season well and heat through.

Drain the pasta, return it to its pan and add the hazelnuts and the contents of the cabbage pan. Season and add the parsley. Drizzle with more olive oil. Serve with grated Parmesan cheese.

new york take-out noodles with cucumber

Something to turn to when you're tired and the cupboard is pretty bare. You can eat it with hot spiced meat – griddled chicken or pork – or just chow down with the noodles in front of the telly. The recipe is from *The New York Times* and is based on a dish made by Shorty Tang at the Hwa Yuan restaurant on East Broadway. As with many Asian dishes, the art is in balance. The sesame sauce needs to be hot, sweet, salty and a tiny bit sour. Sometimes I add sliced radishes to the cucumber, soaking the radishes in iced water to give a really good crunch; it's a great contrast to the soft noodles. There are lots of chilli-garlic pastes on the market and they vary a lot in heat, so add it to taste. I prefer to use a Chinese variety for this, such as Sichuan chilli bean paste, but you could also use sriracha (see page 330 for stockists).

Serves 6

700g (1lb 9oz) medium egg noodles
2 tbsp toasted sesame oil, plus a little more
2 tbsp Chinese sesame paste (see page 330)
1½ tbsp smooth peanut butter
3½ tbsp dark soy sauce
2 tbsp rice vinegar
1 tbsp soft light brown sugar

1.5cm (½in) root ginger, peeled and finely grated
1 fat garlic clove, finely grated
chilli-garlic paste, to taste (it should be hot)
1 ridge cucumber, peeled and very finely sliced
handful of roasted salted peanuts, chopped
handful of chopped herb leaves, such as mint
   and coriander

Cook the noodles according to the packet instructions, then drain and rinse in cold water. Shake off the excess water in a colander. Put the noodles into a bowl and drizzle with a little toasted sesame oil to stop them sticking together.

Whisk the sesame paste and peanut butter in a bowl (just use a fork), then whisk in the soy sauce, rice vinegar, the 2 tbsp of sesame oil, sugar, ginger, garlic and chilli-garlic paste. Taste and adjust if you need to. It might seem strong, but it's going on to bland noodles. Toss the sauce with the noodles and top with the cucumber, then add the peanuts and herbs.

crab & peas
with casarecce

FOR A RICHER DISH, add 3 tbsp of cream to the crab before you toss it with the pasta. The brown crab meat here intensifies the flavour, even if it does make it look 'muddy', but it's optional. I like the shape of casarecce, but you can use other pasta instead.

SERVES 4

150g (5½oz) casarecce, or other pasta shapes

salt and pepper

100g (3½oz) sugar snap peas

150g (5½oz) fresh or frozen peas (podded weight)

30g (1oz) unsalted butter

1 tbsp olive oil

2 garlic cloves, finely sliced

275g (9¾oz) white crab meat, picked over

50g (1¾oz) brown crab meat (optional)

a couple of generous squeezes of lemon juice

20g (¾oz) pea shoots, coarse stalks removed

Cook the pasta in plenty of boiling lightly salted water until tender but still al dente (this is usually a couple of minutes less than suggested on the packet).

Halve the sugar snaps along their length so you can see the peas peeking out. Put these and the regular peas into a saucepan of boiling water and cook for about two minutes. Meanwhile, heat the butter and oil in a small frying pan and cook the garlic until it's soft. Toss in the crab meat, including the brown meat, if using, and briskly heat. Add salt, pepper and a good squeeze of lemon juice.

Drain the pasta and put it into a warm serving bowl with the drained peas, the crab and all the juices from its pan and the pea shoots. Toss together gently – don't crush the pea shoots – season again, add another good squeeze of lemon juice and serve.

orzo with lemon & parsley

I CAN'T TELL YOU HOW USEFUL this is. When I feel lazy, I make it instead of risotto. It takes – literally – 12 minutes from beginning to end. The result is a creamy dish that is very soothing on its own, or lovely with roast or grilled chicken. Orzo is a pasta that looks like grains of rice. If you're a Parmesan cheese lover you'll adore it, as orzo is pretty much a vehicle for the stuff. Orzo is also great to feed to hungry children as it cooks so quickly and, when you're ill, it's like Italian penicillin in a bowl. It's also the most terrific telly food… snuggle into your sofa with a bowl and eat with a spoon. You can add chopped spinach leaves to this as well. It will just wilt in the heat of the pasta.

SERVES 4 as a side dish, 2 as a main course
½ tbsp olive oil
4 shallots or ½ small onion, finely chopped
1 garlic clove, finely chopped
400ml (14fl oz) light chicken stock
225g (8oz) orzo
finely grated zest of ½ unwaxed lemon
3 tbsp finely chopped parsley leaves
80–100g (3–3½oz) finely grated Parmesan cheese, to taste
salt and pepper

Heat the olive oil and gently sauté the shallots until soft and pale gold. Add the garlic and cook for a further couple of minutes. Add the stock and bring to the boil, then add the orzo.

Increase the heat to medium and cook, uncovered, for eight minutes. You can stir it a couple of times to stop the pasta sticking, but try not to do so too much. By the end the stock should have been absorbed and the pasta become soft, but still with a little firmness.

Stir in the lemon zest, parsley and Parmesan cheese. Taste and season; you won't need much salt, if any, because of the reduced stock and the cheese. Eat promptly; it gets sticky if it's kept waiting, although it does – amazingly – reheat well if you do it gently with a little more stock.

fettuccine with asparagus, peas & saffron

RATHER CHIC, and a bit of a treat if there's just two of you. Shreds of Parma ham, flaked cooked salmon or – if you're pushing the boat out – seared scallops are all lovely additions. Just toss them with the cream and the vegetables.

SERVES 2

generous pinch of saffron stamens

15g (½oz) unsalted butter

2 shallots, finely chopped

100ml (3½fl oz) vermouth

250ml (9fl oz) chicken or vegetable stock

100ml (3½fl oz) double cream

salt and pepper

lemon juice

180g (6oz) fresh fettuccine

200g (7oz) asparagus tips

175g (6oz) peas

finely grated Parmesan or pecorino cheese, to serve

Put the saffron in a cup and stir in 50ml (2fl oz) of boiling water. Set aside for 30 minutes.

For the sauce, melt the butter in a saucepan and cook the shallots until soft but not coloured. Add the vermouth and boil until it has reduced to about 50ml (2fl oz). Add the saffron water and stock and boil until reduced by two-thirds. Add the cream and bring to the boil. Season and boil until the sauce can coat the back of a spoon. Add a little lemon juice and check the seasoning.

Cook the pasta in boiling lightly salted water until al dente, about a minute or so less than suggested on the packet instructions. When it is nearly ready, steam the asparagus tips until just tender (test with the tip of a knife), boil the peas for three minutes and drain. Drain the pasta and toss quickly with the vegetables and sauce. Serve with grated Parmesan or pecorino cheese.

turkish pasta with feta, yogurt & dill

TURKISH MANTI – lamb-filled pasta shapes – are served with yogurt sauce. They're laborious to make, but I love the basic idea of pasta with yogurt and feta and so I came up with this instead. It takes a while for the onions to caramelize but you can pretty much leave them to cook.

SERVES 2

425g (15oz) onions (about 4 medium onions), very finely sliced

2 tbsp olive oil

1 bay leaf

5cm (2in) piece of cinnamon stick

1 garlic clove, crushed

salt and pepper

1 tsp caster sugar (optional)

squeeze of lemon juice (optional)

145g (5¼oz) tagliatelle

50g (1¾oz) Greek yogurt

1½ tbsp milk or buttermilk

2 tbsp chopped dill fronds

15g (½oz) unsalted butter

¼ tsp cayenne pepper

finely crumbled feta cheese, to serve

Put the onions in a heavy-based pan with the olive oil, bay and cinnamon. Cook over a medium heat, stirring, until the onions are starting to turn golden, then add the garlic and cook for a further two minutes. Add a splash of water, cover the pan, reduce the heat right down and leave until the onions are almost caramelized, about 35 minutes. Check on them every so often to give them a stir and ensure they're not getting too dry.

When the onions are totally soft, remove the lid, season and boil until any excess liquid has evaporated. (If they haven't caramelized very well you could add the 1 tsp of sugar, but balance it by adding a good squeeze of lemon juice, too.)

Cook the tagliatelle until al dente in boiling salted water, usually a couple of minutes less than suggested on the packet. When it is almost ready, add the yogurt and milk or buttermilk to the onions and heat, but don't boil. Drain the pasta and toss it into the onion pan with the dill.

Quickly melt the butter in a small saucepan and add the cayenne. Cook for about 20 seconds. Serve the pasta with the spiced butter drizzled on top and offer the feta cheese on the side.

black linguine with squid & spicy sausage

BLACK PASTA is easier to find than it was. Its main advantage is that it looks so dramatic, especially if you serve something white – squid, prawns or scallops – with it (all are good here), but you can of course use regular pasta. Don't add too much parsley, as it can dominate. Look for spicy Italian sausages in a good deli, though supermarkets sell spicy sausages, usually smoky Spanish-flavoured varieties, which work, too.

SERVES 2

150g (5½oz) black linguine or spaghetti
salt and pepper
300g (10½oz) squid, cleaned
150g (5½oz) spicy sausage
3 tbsp olive oil
2 garlic cloves, finely sliced

1 red chilli, deseeded and finely chopped
1 tbsp finely chopped flat leaf parsley leaves
juice of ½ lemon
extra virgin olive oil, to serve

Cook the pasta in plenty of boiling lightly salted water according to the packet instructions. Meanwhile, get on with the squid and sausage.

Cut the wings off the squid. If they are large, cut them into three or four strips, but it's usually fine just to halve them. Slice the bodies down one side, then cut into 1.5cm (½in) strips. Separate the tentacles, halving if they're big. Blot the squid with kitchen paper: if it's wet it won't fry well.

Remove the casing from the sausage and break the meat into little nuggets a bit bigger than a pea. Heat 1 tbsp of the regular olive oil in a large frying pan or a wok and cook the sausagemeat over a fairly high heat until browned all over. Lift out with a slotted spoon and set aside. Add the rest of the regular olive oil and increase the heat to high. When it is very hot, throw in the squid and cook for about a minute, then add the garlic, chilli, seasoning and the sausage. Toss it around for another 30–40 seconds (you want the garlic to be pale gold, but not to burn).

Throw in the parsley and squeeze on the lemon juice. Quickly drain the pasta and throw it into the pan. Toss everything around, add a good slug of extra virgin olive oil and serve immediately.

linguine all'amalfitana

I'M ALWAYS LOOKING for new simple pasta dishes and southern Italy is a great hunting ground. Anchovies and walnuts seems like an odd pairing, but it works well.

SERVES 2

165g (5¾oz) linguine
salt and pepper
3 tbsp extra virgin olive oil, plus more to serve (optional)
2 garlic cloves, crushed
½ tsp chilli flakes
50g (1¾oz) walnuts, roughly chopped
8 really good-quality cured anchovies, roughly chopped
finely grated pecorino cheese, to serve (optional)

Cook the linguine in boiling salted water until al dente, usually a couple of minutes less than it says on the packet instructions.

Meanwhile, heat the olive oil in a sauté pan or a shallow casserole and gently fry the garlic, chilli flakes and nuts for a few minutes. Don't let the garlic brown. Add the anchovies and press them down in the pan with the back of a wooden spoon; they'll melt in the heat.

Add three-quarters of a cup of the pasta cooking water to the anchovy pan, then drain the pasta and add that to the pan, too. Cook the pasta in the sauté pan for a couple of minutes. The cooking water will reduce to form a sauce with the other ingredients and the pasta will become glossy. Season.

You can add another slug of extra virgin olive oil, if you want. Serve with grated pecorino cheese, or without any cheese at all.

pasta all'ortolana

QUITE CLEVER THIS, basically a carbonara made with courgettes. I use
a fairly high proportion of vegetables to pasta because I like it that way,
but increase the quantity of spaghetti if you want.

SERVES 4

300g (10½oz) spaghetti

salt and pepper

400g (14oz) courgettes

4 tbsp extra virgin olive oil

1 small onion, very finely sliced

1 garlic clove, very finely sliced

2 eggs, plus 4 egg yolks

100g (3½oz) finely grated Parmesan cheese

50g (1¾oz) finely grated pecorino cheese

leaves from a small bunch of basil, torn

Cook the spaghetti in a large pan of boiling lightly salted water until it is al dente (usually a
couple of minutes less than it says on the packet).

Meanwhile, trim the tops and bases of the courgettes and cut the flesh into strips (somewhere
between matchsticks and batons). Heat the olive oil in a large frying pan and sauté the
courgettes and onion over a medium-high heat (you'll need to reduce it after a while), until
golden all over and cooked through. Add the garlic and cook for another minute.

In a bowl, beat the eggs, yolks and both cheeses well, seasoning with lots of pepper.

When the pasta is al dente, drain, reserving half a cup of the cooking water. Pour the reserved
pasta water into the courgettes. Now add the spaghetti to the pan and stir it with the vegetables,
leaving it over the heat for a few moments to allow some of the water to evaporate and the pasta
to absorb the flavours.

Working quickly, take the pan off the heat and stir in the egg and cheese mixture, moving
everything around until every strand of pasta is coated and the sauce has thickened: the eggs
shouldn't scramble, instead the sauce should just thicken. Taste. Add more salt if it needs it,
throw on the basil and serve immediately.

pâtes à la cévenole

THIS RECIPE IS FROM SOUTHERN FRANCE and, if you like
comforting bowls of pasta, it's a stunner. Don't be put off by the
chestnuts, they really make the dish. You can buy them frozen or
vacuum-packed very easily.

SERVES 6
200g (7oz) small macaroni
salt and pepper
400g (14oz) chestnut mushrooms, or other mushrooms if you can't find those
1 tbsp olive oil
15g (½oz) unsalted butter
½ garlic clove, finely chopped
125g (4½oz) cooked chestnuts, very roughly chopped
500ml (18fl oz) double cream
freshly grated nutmeg
75g (2¾oz) Gruyère cheese, grated

Put the macaroni into a large pot of boiling lightly salted water and cook until al dente (usually
a couple of minutes less than it says on the packet). Preheat the oven to 190°C/375°F/gas mark 5.

Get on with the rest of the dish while the pasta is cooking. Slice the mushrooms quite thickly
and sauté them in the olive oil over a fairly high heat until golden brown. You want a good
colour here. (You may have to do it in batches, there's a lot of mushrooms.) They throw out a lot
of water and you have to drive this off, or you'll end up with grey liquid when the dish is baked.

Add the butter to the mushrooms – it's great for flavour – plus the garlic, chestnuts and
seasoning. Drain the pasta and add it, too. Pour in the cream, grate in the nutmeg (be
generous) and bring to the boil. Check the seasoning again.

Transfer immediately to a gratin dish and sprinkle the cheese on top. Cook in the oven for
45 minutes. It should be golden and bubbling and the cream should have reduced. Serve with
a baby spinach or watercress salad.

pasta master

AUGUST IN ROME. I'm sitting in a quiet trattoria in the suburbs. It has taken an hour to get here in the sweltering heat but it's worth it: the place is famous for its fritti – arancini, courgette flowers stuffed with cheese and anchovies – and its pasta.

As soon as the carbonara, a dish in which eggs are cooked just enough by strands of hot spaghetti to form a 'sauce' (but not so much that they scramble) arrives, I am completely content. I'm also reminded how good something this ordinary and inexpensive – only the nuggets of salty guanciale with which the dish is studded cost much – can be. It isn't just the flavour, it's the fact that it's soft, that there is a ritual to eating it – twirling it round your fork – that it can be made quickly and with a little style.

I watch the Italians around me eating small platefuls of pasta as a precursor to their *pollo alla diavola* or veal chop… and think of my favourite pasta photographs, of Maria Callas and a group of her girlfriends eating pasta on a train in 1955 on the way to La Scala, of Sophia Loren looking for all the world as if pasta had created every wonderful curve on her body. They are all eating with such joy, heads held back and mouths wide open, as though a love of pasta exhibits a love of life itself.

Most of us, in contrast, have come to regard pasta not as a joy, but as a filler. It's the convenience food par excellence; it's easy and nearly every child will eat it. God knows what we did before supermarkets were full of packets of tubes, strands, shells, corkscrews and butterflies. Familiarity has, to a certain extent, bred contempt.

For a start, we don't prepare it well. Pasta has to be cooked in plenty of boiling salted water (1 litre/1¾ pints for every 100g/3½oz of pasta). Dress it with melted butter or olive oil if your sauce isn't ready and, when saucing, don't overdo it; the pasta, with its own flavour and texture, is just as important as the sauce. Remember that the sauce should just coat the pasta, not drown it. Adding a little of the cooking water from the pasta to the sauce loosens it, and helps both pasta and sauce to combine well.

Tossed with cream, lemon zest and shreds of Parma ham, or with wild mushrooms and truffles, pasta can be luxurious, but more often it allows you to revel in the frugal… and also to cook spontaneously. I feel a little rise of pleasure as I spot a bunch of parsley that can be tossed with spaghetti, extra virgin olive oil and dried chilli. Carrying a big bowl of this to the table makes me happy: I've taken ordinary ingredients and turned them into something good.

Frugal, simple, generous, these are some of the best attributes a dish can have (in my book, anyway). Pasta, if cooked with care and approached with verve, can be all these things, something that Maria Callas and Sophia Loren knew well.

smoky couscous

You can extend this: add cooked chickpeas or black beans, sautéing them in a little olive oil if you want to serve the dish hot; or baby spinach leaves. It's great with pork (try it with Spanish spiced pork with sherried onions, see page 170), lamb, or 'meaty' fish such as monkfish. I also like it with fried tomatoes and chopped chillies tossed in, topped with a fried egg. Couscous is not a grain – it's made from little pellets of rolled semolina – but is treated as one, which is why it is in this chapter. It's a boon, as it's so quick to prepare. And the riffs on it (it goes as well with cool dill as with hot chilli and smoky paprika) are endless.

Serves 6–8 as a side dish

200g (7oz) couscous
300ml (½ pint) boiling chicken or vegetable
   stock, or just boiling water
4 tbsp olive oil
1 large onion, very finely sliced
2 garlic cloves, finely chopped
1½ tsp smoked paprika
juice of ½ lemon
2 tbsp extra virgin olive oil

85g (3oz) pitted green olives, roughly chopped
20g (¾oz) smoked almonds, roughly chopped
a few roasted red peppers from a jar, torn or
   chopped (optional)
leaves from a small bunch of coriander, chopped
salt and pepper

Sprinkle the couscous into a bowl, pour over the hot stock or water and add half the regular olive oil. Cover with cling film and leave for 15 minutes.

Heat the remaining regular olive oil in a frying pan and sauté the onion over a medium heat until soft and golden. Add the garlic and smoked paprika and cook for a further minute.

Fork the couscous through: it should be fluffy, not wet (if it's dry, add no more than 50ml/2fl oz extra stock or water and leave for a little longer). Fork the onion mixture into the couscous. Add the lemon juice, extra virgin olive oil, olives, almonds, peppers (if using) and coriander. Season.

Gently toss together and serve warm or at room temperature.

spelt with blackberries, beets, walnuts & buttermilk

I STARTED OUT MAKING a Scandinavian-influenced dish here – spelt, berries and buttermilk are such northern ingredients – but because blackberries are so loved in Georgia I went off on another tack, adding spices and heat. You can leave the spices out – or use more Scandi flavours, caraway for example – depending on what you want to serve it with. It's surprisingly good with salmon and mackerel.

SERVES 6–8 as a side dish
150g (5½oz) pearled spelt
2½ tbsp olive oil
juice of ½ lemon
1 tsp white balsamic vinegar
salt and pepper
½ red onion, very finely sliced
1 tsp ground coriander
1 tsp cayenne pepper
35g (1¼oz) walnut pieces
2 cooked beetroots, cut into matchsticks

150g (5½oz) blackberries
1 tbsp chopped dill fronds
1 tbsp chopped coriander leaves

For the dressing
200ml (7fl oz) buttermilk
smidgen of Dijon mustard
pinch of caster sugar
1 garlic clove, crushed
2 tbsp extra virgin olive oil

Cook the spelt in boiling water until tender (20–25 minutes, but check the packet instructions). Drain and run cold water through it. Shake off the excess water and put into a serving bowl with 2 tbsp of the regular olive oil, the lemon juice, vinegar and seasoning.

Make the buttermilk dressing by mixing everything together. Taste for seasoning.

Heat the rest of the regular olive oil and cook the onion until it has just lost its rawness, then add the spices and cook for another two minutes. Add this to the spelt, then toast the walnut pieces in the same pan for a minute or so, until they smell aromatic. Tip them into the bowl along with all the other ingredients and gently toss together.

Drizzle with some of the buttermilk dressing (offer the rest in a jug) and serve.

eastern black rice, mango & tomatoes with coconut

BLACK 'VENUS' RICE – I apologize for the high-falutin' name – is a new discovery for me. It's not like sticky Asian black rice, as the grains stay separate and nutty. I adore it. It looks spectacular with bright colours. You can get the coconut flesh for this in little tubs now, you don't have to buy a whole coconut.

SERVES 6–8 as a side dish

For the salad
300g (10½oz) black 'venus' rice
1 mango, just ripe or slightly under-ripe
100g (3½oz) sugar snap peas
15g (½oz) basil leaves
leaves from 10 sprigs of mint
200g (7oz) well-flavoured tomatoes, chopped
2 red and 1 green chilli, deseeded and shredded
2 spring onions, trimmed and finely chopped
30g (1oz) roasted salted peanuts, chopped
40g (1½oz) fresh coconut flesh, shaved

For the dressing
finely grated zest and juice of 2 limes
1 garlic clove, finely grated
2cm (¾in) piece of root ginger, peeled and finely grated
2 tbsp groundnut oil
1½ tbsp fish sauce
2½ tbsp caster sugar

Put the rice into a saucepan of boiling water, then reduce the heat to a good, vigorous simmer. Cook until tender, though it retains a 'bite'. It takes about 45 minutes. Drain and rinse under cold water until the water runs clear; this rice stains, so you need to get the excess colour out.

Peel the mango and cut the 'cheeks' off each side (the bits lying right next to the stone). Cut really close to the stone so that you remove the plumpest bit of the mango you can. Carefully remove the other bits of flesh; you can't use any here that is soft or bruised, so keep that for a smoothie. Cut into chunks about 1cm (½in) square.

Shred the sugar snaps lengthways. To make the dressing, just mix everything together; it will taste quite tart. Tear the larger basil and mint leaves, leaving the small leaves intact.

Gently mix the dressing with all the ingredients, except the peanuts and coconut, in a broad shallow bowl where you can see all the colours. Scatter with the peanuts and coconut and serve.

smoked haddock, barley & spinach salad

IF YOU WANT to make this more substantial, a poached egg is lovely on top.
Spelt or farro can be used instead of barley, just cook them in the same way.

SERVES 6

For the dressing
25ml (1fl oz) Dijon mustard
4 tbsp white wine vinegar
salt and pepper
1 tsp caster sugar
180ml (6fl oz) light and fruity
  extra virgin olive oil
75ml (2½fl oz) single cream

For the salad
225g (8oz) pearl barley
2 tbsp olive oil
good squeeze of lemon juice
1 tbsp chopped parsley leaves
1kg (2lb 4oz) undyed smoked haddock fillet,
  cut into 6 portions
25g (¾oz) unsalted butter
1 tbsp sunflower oil
350g (12oz) baby spinach leaves

To make the dressing, put the mustard, vinegar, seasoning and sugar into a small jug and gradually add the extra virgin olive oil, whisking with a fork as you do so. Whisk in the cream and taste for seasoning. Set aside.

Cook the barley in boiling lightly salted water until tender, about 30 minutes. Drain, rinse in warm water and drain again, shaking out any excess liquid. Transfer to a warm bowl and stir in the regular olive oil, lemon juice, parsley and seasoning. Cover and keep warm.

Make sure there are no little bones in the fish by rubbing your hands over the surface. Divide the butter and sunflower oil between two frying pans and cook three pieces of fish in each, flesh side down first, over a medium heat until pale gold underneath (about two minutes). Carefully turn the fish over, reduce the heat a little and cover both pans. Cook for about five minutes, or until the flesh is opaque. Take the pans off the heat.

Divide the spinach between six plates with the barley. Lift the fish from its skin – I use a knife and fork – trying to keep it in fairly big chunks. Put it on the salad and spoon over the dressing.

spelt with carrots & kale

SIDE DISHES get a rather bad deal in cookery books, though an array of good sides are a real boon. Use cavolo nero if you prefer it to kale.

SERVES 6 as a side dish
30g (1oz) unsalted butter
1 small onion, very finely chopped
3 carrots, peeled and finely chopped
300g (10½oz) pearled spelt
600ml (1 pint) light chicken stock
300g (10½oz) kale, coarse ribs discarded, leaves roughly chopped
salt and pepper

Melt 10g (¼oz) of the butter in a saucepan and add the onion and carrots. Sauté over a medium heat until soft but not coloured. Add the spelt and stir around in the fat. Pour on the stock, bring to the boil, then reduce the heat to a simmer. Gently simmer for about 30 minutes. It will become tender – though it will retain a little 'bite' in the middle of each grain – and should have absorbed all the stock. Take off the heat and cover to keep warm.

Put the kale in a saucepan and add enough boiling water to cover. Cook for five minutes over a medium heat, then drain and squeeze out any excess water with your hands. Put it into a small pan with the rest of the butter, season and sauté for a few minutes until some of the moisture has evaporated. Stir into the warm spelt. Serve immediately.

bacon & egg risotto

RATHER ANNOYINGLY I'm asking for 700ml (1¼ pints) of stock here, when supermarkets sell 500ml tubs. If you aren't using home-made stock you can actually use a 500ml tub here and make up the remaining quantity with water. You're reducing the stock as it cooks in the risotto, so you'll still end up with a good flavour. If you like the comfort of poached eggs (and who doesn't?) you will love this. Poached eggs + risotto = bliss.

SERVES 2

700ml (1¼ pints) chicken stock
15g (½oz) unsalted butter
150g (5½oz) bacon lardons
1 small onion, finely chopped
150g (5½oz) risotto rice
pepper
2 tbsp finely chopped parsley leaves
25g (scant 1oz) finely grated Parmesan cheese
2 eggs

Heat the stock and keep it simmering while you cook the risotto.

Melt the butter in a heavy-based saucepan and sauté the bacon until golden all over, then stir in the onion. Cook over a medium heat until the onion is soft and pale gold. Add the rice, turning it over in the fat and juices, and cook for a couple of minutes until it is translucent.

Add the stock a ladle at a time, stirring continuously. Don't add any new stock until the last lot has been absorbed. The rice will soften and become creamy with just a little bite in the centre of each grain. It takes 20–25 minutes. Season with pepper (you shouldn't need salt because of the bacon and stock). Stir in the parsley and half the Parmesan cheese and check the seasoning.

Cover and leave to rest while you quickly poach the eggs (see page 19, or poach them according to your favourite method). Serve an egg on top of each serving of risotto with the remaining Parmesan cheese on the side.

couscous with flowers

DISHES LIKE THIS ARE MAGICAL because you've made some effort
with your shopping, not with your cooking. Often farmer's markets have
stalls selling edible flowers and petals, so see what you can find. Other
edible flowers – such as geraniums, nasturtiums and roses – can be used,
they just have to be unsprayed. See what your neighbours have in their
gardens (but ask, first!).

SERVES 6 as a side dish
200g (7oz) couscous
300ml (½ pint) boiling chicken stock or water, plus more if needed
2 tbsp olive oil
1 small garlic clove, crushed
finely grated zest and juice of 1 unwaxed lemon
3 tbsp extra virgin olive oil
salt and pepper
3 tbsp chopped flat leaf parsley leaves
small handful of torn mint leaves
small handful of purple basil leaves
2 spring onions, trimmed and very finely chopped
handful of pea shoots, any coarse stalks removed
edible flowers, either whole or petals

Sprinkle the couscous into a bowl, then pour over the stock or water and the regular olive oil.
Cover with cling film and leave for 15 minutes. Fork it through every so often to separate and
aerate the grains; it should be fluffy. When the couscous is cool, use your fingers to break down
any little clumps. If it still seems a little dry, add more liquid (no more than 50ml/2fl oz) and
leave it for a little longer.

Add the garlic, lemon zest and juice, extra virgin olive oil and plenty of salt and pepper. Taste
for seasoning. Gently mix in the herbs, spring onions, pea shoots and half the flowers. Place in
a broad serving bowl and scatter the rest of the flowers on top.

FISH

salmon & cucumber with miso dressing

I ONLY STARTED TO COOK with miso a few years ago and am now addicted to its strong flavour. There are lots of types, some quite sweet, others as umami-rich as Marmite. Keep the jar in the fridge once you've opened it and use it within three months. You can make this with tuna, too. Serve it on white or brown rice, or just on its own.

SERVES 2 as a light lunch
150g (5½oz) salmon fillet, skinned
125g (4½oz) cucumber
1 tbsp white miso paste
1 tbsp mirin
1 tbsp light soy sauce
1 tsp rice vinegar
1 tbsp rapeseed or groundnut oil
pinch of caster sugar or smidgen of honey
2 spring onions, trimmed and finely chopped
½ tbsp pickled ginger, finely sliced
1 tsp black or white sesame seeds
micro leaves, such as cress or amaranth, to serve (optional)

Cut the salmon into chubby matchsticks. Halve the cucumber and cut it into matchsticks, too (you don't need to peel it or remove the seeds unless you prefer to).

In a small bowl, mix the miso, mirin, soy sauce, vinegar and oil with the sugar or honey. Toss the salmon and cucumber with this dressing, the spring onions and ginger and divide between two plates.

Sprinkle with sesame seeds and micro leaves, if you have them. Serve.

prawn, fennel & tomato pilaf with mint

A GREAT DISH FOR TWO. Leave the pilaf to cook, then quickly fry the prawns at the last minute. You can use dry white wine if you don't have vermouth… but I always keep vermouth, as it never fails to come in handy and it's so brilliant with fish.

SERVES 2

110g (4oz) basmati rice
½ fennel bulb
3 tbsp olive oil
½ onion, finely chopped
1 garlic clove, finely chopped
good pinch of chilli flakes
150g (5½oz) well-flavoured plum tomatoes, deseeded and roughly chopped

100ml (3½fl oz) dry vermouth
175ml (6fl oz) chicken, fish or vegetable stock
200g (7oz) raw king prawns, shelled and deveined
salt and pepper
2 tbsp finely chopped mixed parsley and mint leaves
50g (1¾oz) feta cheese, crumbled

Put the rice into a sieve and rinse it until the water runs clear.

Halve the fennel and remove the outer layer of leaves – they're usually a bit discoloured – and the tips, but keep any little fronds. Cut out the core of each piece and discard; chop the flesh.

Heat half the olive oil and sauté the fennel and onion until soft but not coloured. Add the garlic and chilli and cook for another couple of minutes, then add the tomatoes. Cook for another two minutes. Add the rice and gently combine everything. Pour in the vermouth and boil until the liquid has reduced by half, then add the stock and return to the boil. Reduce the heat right down and cook for 20 minutes, until the rice is tender and the liquid has been absorbed.

When it's almost ready, heat the rest of the oil in a small frying pan and cook the prawns until they turn pink. Season. Gently fork the herbs and prawns through the rice and sprinkle on the feta. Serve immediately.

salmon, fennel & potatoes en papillote with dill butter

THE COOKING TIME will vary depending on the thickness of the fish you use. If you have those chunky fillets (the type most often sold in supermarkets in packs of two or four), the timings here work perfectly. Thinner pieces will cook more quickly. This is good with the crème fraîche sauce on page 133.

SERVES 4

300g (10½oz) small, waxy potatoes
½ small fennel bulb
40g (1½oz) unsalted butter, melted
8 sprigs of dill, fronds from half of
them chopped

salt and pepper
4 fillets of salmon (thick centre pieces),
about 140g (5oz) each
4 tbsp dry white vermouth

Cook the potatoes in boiling water until they are softening, but not completely tender through to the centre. Drain and cut into slices about the thickness of a 50p coin.

Trim any little fronds you find on the fennel and reserve. Halve the bulb and remove the outer leaves if discoloured or very coarse. Cut out the core from each piece. Cut the fennel into slices (it's best to do this with a mandolin if you have one, but a sharp knife will do).

Preheat the oven to 200°C/400°F/gas mark 6. Cut out eight rectangles of greaseproof or baking parchment, each roughly 40 x 37cm (16 x 15in). Two pieces will go together to make each parcel. Set the four double-thickness rectangles of baking parchment on a work surface and brush their middles with butter. Divide the potatoes and fennel between them, layering with the chopped dill and seasoning and drizzling with a little butter as you go. Put the salmon on top, season and pour on the rest of the butter. Add a splash of vermouth and a whole sprig of dill to each. Carefully pull the doubled baking parchment layers up and over the fish, turning them to seal the edges; don't roll them up tightly, you want to make a kind of tent. Seal each parcel by screwing the ends as if making crackers.

Put the parcels on a baking sheet and cook for 25 minutes. Unwrap at the table to serve.

bream stuffed with walnuts & pomegranates

SO EASY you can have it midweek (what a treat), but special enough to give to friends at the weekend, too. Get a pot of pomegranate seeds if you don't have time to extract them from the fruit. Serve with couscous or grains. Spelt with blackberries, beets, walnuts & buttermilk (see page 112) would be gorgeous alongside, but leave out the blackberries.

SERVES 4

4 bream (about 350g/12oz each), cleaned, trimmed and scaled
salt and pepper
3 small garlic cloves, finely chopped
1 dried red chilli, crumbled
100g (3½oz) walnuts, roughly chopped, plus a few more, toasted (see page 112), to serve
4 tbsp extra virgin olive oil, plus more to cook and serve
juice of ½ lemon, plus lemon wedges to serve
2 tsp pomegranate molasses
2 tsp honey
30g (1oz) coriander leaves, finely chopped
100g (3½oz) pomegranate seeds, plus more to serve

Preheat the oven to 200°C/400°F/gas mark 6. Make two diagonal cuts in the flesh of the fish on each side. Season their insides. Mix the rest of the ingredients together and season. Put this mixture inside each fish and lay them in a lightly oiled roasting tin, or in two separate oiled roasting tins. Season the outside of the fish and drizzle with olive oil.

Cook in the oven for 20 minutes, then check the fish at their thickest parts. The flesh should be white, not glassy. If they aren't yet ready, return them to the oven for another four minutes or so.

Scatter with toasted walnuts and pomegranate seeds, drizzle with olive oil and serve immediately with lemon wedges.

cod with a crab
& herb crust

YOU NEED BITS OF COD all the same size for this, so they're perfectly cooked together. It's best with chunky fillets, rather than thinner pieces (the cooking time here is for thicker bits). You don't have to do the sauce – it can feel like a hassle when you haven't got much time – but it makes the dish a little more special if you're giving it to friends at the weekend.

SERVES 6

For the cod
olive oil, for the tin
6 x 150g (5½oz) thick fillets of cod
salt and pepper
300g (10½oz) white crab meat, picked over
150g (5½oz) fresh white breadcrumbs
finely grated zest and juice of 1 unwaxed lemon,
    plus lemon wedges to serve
75g (2¾oz) unsalted butter, melted
leaves from 4 sprigs of tarragon, chopped
2 tbsp finely chopped chives
½ tbsp finely chopped parsley leaves

For the sauce
100g (3½oz) crème fraîche
2 tbsp mayonnaise
30g (1oz) watercress leaves, coarse stalks
    removed, chopped
1 shallot, finely chopped
½ tsp Dijon mustard
1 tbsp capers, rinsed of salt or brine, chopped
squeeze of lemon juice

Preheat the oven to 200°C/400°F/gas mark 6. Lightly oil a roasting tin. Put the fillets into it and season them. Mix all the other ingredients together, season and divide between the fillets, patting the mixture gently down on top of each piece.

Mix together everything for the sauce and season well.

Cook the fish in the oven for 14–15 minutes. Serve with the sauce and lemon wedges, with green beans, boiled waxy potatoes and a green vegetable or watercress salad alongside.

devilled mackerel with watercress yogurt

GRILLS VARY A LOT and this cooking time works for my grill, which does get very hot. You might have to increase the time, but be careful not to burn the fish skin; instead move the grill pan away from the heating element if you have to.

SERVES 6

6 whole mackerel, cleaned and trimmed, about 275g (9¾oz) each

125g (4½oz) unsalted butter, softened

2 tsp cayenne pepper

1 tsp ground ginger

½ tsp chilli flakes

2 tsp ground coriander

3 tsp caster sugar

2 tsp English mustard

3 tsp red wine vinegar

good squeeze of lemon juice

salt and pepper

300g (10½oz) Greek yogurt

½ cucumber, peeled, halved, deseeded and chopped

handful of watercress, coarse stalks discarded, chopped

Preheat the grill on its highest setting. Make three slashes in each of the mackerel on both sides. Mix the butter with the spices, sugar, mustard, vinegar and lemon juice (it works best to just mash it with a fork). Season. Rub this all over the mackerel, including inside their bodies.

Place the mackerel on a grill tray covered with foil (it just makes for easier cleaning) and grill for four minutes on each side, or until cooked through. Mix the yogurt with the cucumber, watercress and seasoning. Serve the yogurt with the mackerel.

miso & soy
glazed mackerel

IF YOU CAN'T BUY really fresh mackerel for this – from a good
fishmonger – then make something else. Mackerel deteriorates
more quickly than any other fish I know. This is very simple and, as
long as you have the ingredients, easy to put together. Use sriracha
or another chilli sauce in the glaze if you don't have fresh chilli.
Serve with boiled rice and stir-fried greens.

SERVES 4

2 tbsp sake

2 tbsp mirin

2 tbsp white miso paste

3 tsp caster sugar

3 tsp soy sauce

2 red chillies, deseeded and finely chopped

2 small garlic cloves, crushed

2 tsp peeled and finely grated root ginger

4 mackerel fillets

2 spring onions, trimmed and chopped on the diagonal

sesame seeds, to serve

Mix all the ingredients – except the fish, spring onions and sesame seeds – in a shallow dish.
Add the fish and turn to coat. Cover and refrigerate for at least one and up to six hours.

Preheat the grill. Remove the fish from the marinade and put it on a foil-lined baking sheet
(or grill pan, the foil just saves on the washing up). Position the fish about 15cm (6in) from
the heat source and cook until just opaque in the centre, about six minutes, then transfer to
warm plates. Sprinkle with the spring onions and sesame seeds and serve.

trofie with courgettes, prawns & chilli

SIMPLE, QUICK AND BIG ON FLAVOUR. And it's one of those dishes – I think it's the prawns and vermouth – that makes you feel as if you're eating it on holiday. It's important to cook the courgettes until they are lovely and golden, that's what will transform quite ordinary ingredients into a really good meal.

SERVES 2

140g (5oz) trofie or casarecce, or any other pasta shape
salt and pepper
3 tbsp extra virgin olive oil
250g (9oz) courgettes, cut into little cubes
1 garlic clove, crushed
150g packet of raw king prawns, shelled and deveined
good pinch of chilli flakes
4 tbsp dry white vermouth (or white wine will do)
juice of ½ small lemon
1 tbsp chopped dill fronds, or a handful of torn basil leaves

Put the pasta to cook in plenty of boiling lightly salted water until al dente, usually a couple of minutes less than suggested on the packet.

Meanwhile, heat 2 tbsp of the olive oil in a frying pan and quickly sauté the courgettes until they're golden all over and quite soft. Add the garlic, prawns, chilli flakes and seasoning and cook for another minute over a fairly high heat, tossing the prawns around. They will turn pink. Splash in the vermouth and let it bubble away to almost nothing.

Quickly drain the pasta and add it to the frying pan along with the lemon juice and whichever herb you're using. Check for seasoning, add the final 1 tbsp of olive oil and serve immediately. It's not usual – in Italy, at least – to serve grated cheese with seafood (and the dish really doesn't need it), but do so if you want.

seared tuna with preserved lemon, olives & avocado

THIS CAME ABOUT ACCIDENTALLY. I'd made the relish – without the avocado or the lemon – to go with lamb, then used the leftovers with a halved avocado that was lurking in the fridge. Once I'd added slivers of preserved lemon, the combination was perfect. You can use coriander or mint instead of parsley, if you prefer.

SERVES 2

For the fish
2 tuna loin steaks
a little olive oil
lemon wedges, to serve

For the relish
115g (4oz) pitted black olives, roughly chopped
2 red chillies, deseeded and very finely sliced
1 tbsp white balsamic vinegar
juice of ½ lemon

4½ tbsp extra virgin olive oil
2 tbsp chopped flat leaf parsley leaves
1 small garlic clove, grated
1 large avocado, pitted, peeled and chopped
1 preserved lemon, fleshy bits removed and
   discarded, rind cut into shreds
salt and pepper

Bring the fish to room temperature.

To make the relish, gently mix everything together. You shouldn't do this too far in advance or it loses its freshness and gets 'tired' and a bit soft, but let it sit for 15 minutes or so before serving so that the flavours can meld.

Use a cast-iron griddle to cook the fish if you have one, otherwise a good frying pan. Brush each piece of tuna with the regular olive oil and season. Heat the pan until really hot, then cook the tuna for about 1½ minutes each side so that it's still slightly raw in the middle, like a rare steak.

Serve the tuna with generous spoonfuls of the relish alongside and lemon wedges.

portuguese baked hake & potatoes

IT DOESN'T SOUND as if this dish will work, or that it's authentic (potatoes baked with mayonnaise is pretty odd), but I've loved it ever since I first tasted it. I don't make mayonnaise especially for this, it's supposed to be quick and easy. I've even left the skin on the potatoes when pushed. It's rich, so it needs a side dish that will cut through that. I like a chicory salad. Roast tomatoes are good, too.

SERVES 6

650g (1lb 7oz) waxy potatoes, peeled
3 tbsp olive oil
1 large onion, finely sliced
3 garlic cloves, finely chopped
2 tbsp finely chopped parsley leaves

salt and pepper
6 hake fillets, about 150g (5½oz) each, skinned
juice of ½ lemon
235g (8½oz) mayonnaise

Boil the potatoes until tender on the outside, but with a little firmness in the middle. Drain.

Heat 1 tbsp of the olive oil in a frying pan and sauté the onion over a medium heat until soft and pale gold (10–12 minutes). Add the garlic and cook gently for another two minutes. Stir in the parsley and season. Preheat the oven to 180°C/350°F/gas mark 4. Put the fish in a gratin dish and squeeze the lemon juice over. Season, then spoon the onion mixture on top.

Slice the potatoes – a little thicker than a £1 coin – and heat the remaining 2 tbsp of olive oil in the frying pan. Sauté the potatoes (in batches if they don't all fit), seasoning as you do so. You just want to get a little colour on them. Don't worry at all if they break up, it doesn't matter.

Spoon the potatoes on to the fish and onions, then spread the mayonnaise on top. It doesn't have to be thick or even, this is a very forgiving dish.

Bake in the oven for 20 minutes, or until the potato topping is golden. Serve immediately.

salmon with tomatoes, pea & basil purée

THIS COULDN'T BE SIMPLER, but it looks very special. If you don't want the hassle of making the tomato sauce, roast some cherry tomatoes on the vine and serve them alongside instead.

SERVES 4

For the purée
250g (9oz) frozen peas
25g (scant 1oz) unsalted butter
3 tbsp double cream
salt and pepper
30g (1oz) basil leaves
good squeeze of lemon juice

For the salmon
100ml (3½fl oz) extra virgin olive oil (preferably a fruity
    sort from Provence, rather than a grassy Tuscan type)
1 fat garlic clove, skin left on
12 basil leaves
2 plum tomatoes, deseeded and chopped
2 tbsp olive oil
4 x 175g (6oz) fillets of salmon

Start with the purée. Cook the peas in boiling water until tender, then drain, reserving the cooking water. Add the butter and let it melt, then tip into a blender or food processor. Add the cream, seasoning, basil and lemon juice and blend until smooth, pouring in some pea cooking water to get the consistency you want. (You can make this ahead and reheat it at the last minute.)

Put the extra virgin olive oil in a frying pan with the garlic (bash the clove with a rolling pin, but leave the skin on) and heat gently. Take off the heat, add six torn leaves of the basil and a good pinch of salt. Leave for 30 minutes so the flavours can infuse, then remove the basil and garlic. Add the tomatoes. Tear the remaining six basil leaves and add them too, then season.

Heat the regular olive oil in another frying pan. Season the salmon on both sides and cook over a medium heat, flesh side down first, for 90 seconds to two minutes, or until golden. Turn and cook on the other side for the same time. Reduce the heat, cover and cook until it is cooked through but still moist. (How long this takes depends on the thickness of the salmon.)

Quickly reheat the purée while the salmon is cooking. Serve the salmon with the purée and spoon the tomato mixture over the top.

baked sea bass with baby leeks, potatoes, raki & dill

A LARGE WHOLE BASS is impressive but, if you end up having to use smaller fish, remember to reduce the cooking time accordingly, as suggested in the recipe.

SERVES 6

500g (1lb 2oz) waxy potatoes, cut as thick as a 50p coin
finely grated zest of 1 unwaxed lemon
fronds from a generous bunch of dill, very roughly chopped
salt and pepper
extra virgin olive oil
1 large sea bass (about 2.5kg/5lb 8oz) or 2 smaller sea bass (each about 1.2kg/
    2lb 10oz), cleaned, trimmed and scaled
100ml (3½fl oz) raki, or Pernod
350g (12oz) baby leeks

Preheat the oven to 200°C/400°F/gas mark 6.

Spread the potatoes out in a roasting tin with the lemon zest and half the dill. Season and add 2 tbsp of the oil. Turn everything over with your hands.

Make three slashes on each side of the fish. Rub with more olive oil, push more dill down into each slit and season inside and out. Place on the bed of potatoes and put some dill into the belly of the fish, too. Pour on the raki.

Cook for 30 minutes for a large fish, or 20 minutes for smaller fish. (If using smaller fish, cook the potatoes on their own for 10 minutes before adding the fish.) Check it is ready: the flesh near the bone in the thickest part of the fish should be white, not at all 'glassy'. If it is not yet ready, give it five minutes more. About five minutes before you expect the fish to be ready, steam or microwave the baby leeks until tender. Drizzle them with oil and season.

Move the fish and potatoes carefully to a warm platter. Arrange the leeks around and serve. Roast tomatoes are good on the side.

pugliese fish tiella

THIS — A LAYERED BAKE of potatoes, pecorino cheese, risotto rice and
fish – is usually made with mussels, but I can't be bothered to prepare those
during the working week. It's a dish I love, though (how could you not like
double carbs baked with pecorino?), so I started to make it with fillets of
fish instead. It's pretty miraculous. Stick the whole dish in the oven and just
wait for it to be transformed.

SERVES 6
extra virgin olive oil
1 large onion, finely sliced
salt and pepper
550g (1lb 4oz) waxy potatoes (no need to peel them; I don't)
400g can of crushed tomatoes
2 tbsp chopped flat leaf parsley leaves
2 garlic cloves, finely chopped
75g (2¾oz) finely grated pecorino cheese (Parmesan if you prefer, but I like pecorino here)
150g (5½oz) arborio rice
4 good-sized fillets of white fish (such as cod, hake or haddock)
300ml (½ pint) fish stock or water

Preheat the oven to 190°C/375°F/gas mark 5.

Drizzle some oil into a baking dish or sauté pan (it must be both oven- and flameproof and
26–30cm / 10–12in diameter) and spread out the onion, seasoning and drizzling with oil.

Either slice or use a mandolin to cut the potatoes really finely. Spread half of these over the
onions, then spoon on half the tomatoes, the parsley, half the garlic and half the pecorino
cheese; season and drizzle with oil as you go. Add the rice and lay the fish on top. Put in the
remaining potatoes, garlic, cheese and tomatoes, in that order. Drizzle on a final bit of oil and
pour in the stock or water.

Bring to the boil on the hob, then immediately transfer to the oven. Bake for 45 minutes, then
check: the potatoes and rice should be tender. If they're not, return to the oven and bake for a
little longer. Serve straight from the dish.

smoked haddock with a mature cheddar crust

A LOVELY AUTUMNAL SUPPER. A salad of baby spinach – with a good mustardy dressing – would be welcome on the side.

SERVES 2

6 tbsp white breadcrumbs

30g (1oz) grated mature Cheddar cheese

½ tbsp finely chopped parsley leaves

1 tbsp olive oil

about 15g (½oz) unsalted butter, melted, plus more for the dish

pepper

2 fillets of smoked haddock, about 175g (6oz) each

Preheat the oven to 220°C/425°F/gas mark 7.

Mix the breadcrumbs, cheese and parsley in a small bowl. Add the oil, melted butter and pepper and mix together.

Lay the fish in a buttered gratin dish where it can lie in a single layer. Pat the breadcrumb crust all over the fish.

Cook for 11–15 minutes (thicker fish fillets will take longer to cook). Check, by poking into the centre of the fish with the tip of a knife, to see whether the fish is cooked right through: cooked fish will have lost that 'glassy' look.

Serve immediately. This is also really good with a purée of peas (just whizz cooked frozen peas with a little chicken stock and a bit of cream or butter). The sweetness of the peas is lovely against the saltiness of the fish.

stir-fried squid with ginger & shaoxing wine

IT'S NOW EASIER to find squid than it used to be. You'll get better stuff at your fishmongers – and he'll prepare it for you – but even supermarket fish counters sell squid whole rather than in those unappetizing looking rings. And it cooks so quickly. Use sherry if you don't have Shaoxing wine.

SERVES 4

900g (2lb) cleaned squid, cut into broad strips

2 lemongrass stalks

1 tbsp groundnut oil

2 garlic cloves, very finely chopped

2cm (¾in) root ginger, peeled and sliced into very fine matchsticks

2–3 red chillies, deseeded and finely chopped

4 spring onions, chopped on the diagonal

1 tsp palm sugar, or caster sugar

salt and pepper

1½ tbsp Shaoxing wine

Pat the squid dry with kitchen paper, otherwise it doesn't fry very well. Remove the tips and coarser outer leaves from the lemongrass and very finely chop the softer inner core.

Heat the oil in a wok and cook the garlic, ginger, chillies and lemongrass for one minute over a low heat (the garlic shouldn't even colour). Whack the heat up high, add the squid and cook for one minute, then add the spring onions, sugar, salt, pepper and wine and cook for another minute. The wine should bubble away to practically nothing. Serve immediately.

simple goan fish curry

I KNOW, I KNOW, Indian dishes can have a long list of ingredients.
But the hardest thing here is getting the spices out of the cupboard.
After that it's a doddle, even on busy nights.

SERVES 4

4 tsp coriander seeds

1 tsp cumin seeds

4 dried red Kashmiri chillies

2cm (¾in) root ginger, peeled and finely grated

4 garlic cloves, crushed

1 tsp ground turmeric

salt and pepper

2 tbsp sunflower or rapeseed oil

1 onion, finely chopped

1 large plum tomato, finely chopped

400ml can of coconut milk

1 tbsp palm sugar, or soft light brown sugar

2 tsp tamarind paste

1 green chilli, deseeded and finely sliced

500g (1lb 2oz) firm white fish fillets, skinned, cut into 3cm (1¼in) chunks

2 tbsp chopped coriander leaves

Toast the coriander and cumin seeds and dried chillies in a dry frying pan for about a minute.
Crush in a mortar and pestle, then mix in the ginger, garlic, turmeric and 1 tsp of salt.

Heat the oil in a sauté pan over a medium heat and fry the onion until soft and golden. Stir
in the spice mix. Cook for a couple of minutes, then add the tomato and cook until it is soft.
Add the coconut milk, sugar, tamarind and green chilli and bring to just under the boil.
Immediately reduce the heat and simmer for about five minutes, until slightly thickened.
Taste for seasoning.

Season the fish all over, then add it to the sauce and simmer gently for about four minutes until
cooked through. Check again for seasoning. Add the coriander leaves and serve with rice.

smoked mackerel with potatoes, eggs & dill pickles

SMOKED MACKEREL makes a really easy supper, but you need to start with good fish for a truly excellent meal. Supermarket offerings vary a lot in quality. I get mine from the fishmonger, if I can. Good smoked mackerel is soft and golden, not firm and dark in colour.

SERVES 4
300g (10½oz) small waxy potatoes (no need to peel)
4 eggs
1½ tbsp extra virgin olive oil (fruity, not grassy)
good squeeze of lemon juice
1 shallot, finely sliced
55g (2oz) sweet pickled cucumber, sliced or chopped
fronds from a small bunch of dill, chopped
salt and pepper
4 heaped tbsp mayonnaise
4 tbsp buttermilk
4 fillets of smoked mackerel

Cook the potatoes in boiling water until tender, then drain. Hard-boil the eggs (cook them in boiling water for seven minutes), then put them in cold water. Halve, quarter or slice the potatoes and put them in a bowl with the olive oil, lemon juice, shallot, pickled cucumber, half the dill and some seasoning. Separately mix together the mayonnaise and buttermilk.

Shell the eggs while they are still warm, quarter them, put them on top of the potatoes and spoon half the buttermilk dressing over everything. Sprinkle with some more dill and add the rest to the remaining dressing. Serve the extra dressing with the salad. Put the smoked mackerel fillets on top, either in one piece or in large flakes.

a bit on the side: sauces and relishes

Mostly we think about food in terms of 'blocks': a plate of roast vegetables, a seared fish steak, a few griddled chops. The question is how, *easily*, to make those blocks special. Simple accessories, delicious 'bits on the side' – butters, relishes and sauces – help you to make them into a meal.

PINE NUT & ANCHOVY CREAM
Good with roast veg, purple-sprouting broccoli, drizzled on kale, or roast or griddled chicken or lamb. Whizz a 50g can of anchovies in oil with 70g (2½oz) toasted pine nuts and 1 crushed garlic clove in a food processor, adding 100ml (3½fl oz) extra virgin olive oil and the juice of ½ lemon. Season with pepper; stir in a few tbsp of finely chopped parsley.

HERB, CAPER & SHALLOT CRÈME FRAÎCHE
A kind of béarnaise substitute (as long as you get tarragon in there). Serve with hard-boiled eggs, poached chicken, roast salmon, lamb and steak. To 200g (7oz) crème fraîche add the chopped leaves from 2 sprigs of tarragon, some finely chopped parsley and chives, 2 tbsp rinsed capers, 1 chopped shallot, 1 tbsp extra virgin olive oil and lemon juice, to taste.

ANCHOVY & ROSEMARY SAUCE
Great with fish (bass, bream, mullet or tuna), roast lamb, bitter leaves such as radicchio, or beans. Pound 1 tsp rosemary leaves in a mortar with 6 chopped anchovies to a rough paste. Add the juice of ½ lemon, then gradually add 2½ tbsp extra virgin olive oil and some pepper.

COCONUT & CORIANDER RELISH
This brings a taste of India to roast chicken or fish, or roast cauliflower and carrots. I can eat it straight, by the spoonful. Into a food processor, put ½ tsp toasted cumin seeds, 25g (scant 1oz) coriander leaves, 50g (1¾oz) grated creamed coconut from a block, 1 deseeded green chilli, 1 chopped garlic clove, the finely grated zest and juice of 1 lime, salt and 1½ tsp caster sugar. Whizz to a purée and taste. Chill.

SPICED HERB YOGURT

Toast ½ tsp each cumin and coriander seeds in a dry frying pan. Crush roughly. Finely chop 10g (¼oz) coriander leaves and the leaves from 10 sprigs of mint. Stir into 250g (9oz) Greek yogurt with the juice of ½ lemon, 4 tbsp extra virgin olive oil and 3 tbsp of water. Lovely with roast or griddled lamb, chicken or pork.

PISTACHIO & FETA PESTO

Put 20g (¾oz) each of pistachio nuts and toasted pumpkin seeds, a 60g (2¼oz) bunch of coriander, 2 chopped garlic cloves, the juice of 2 limes, 1 deseeded green chilli and seasoning into a food processor. Blitz, adding 125ml (4fl oz) extra virgin olive oil. Stir in 60g (2¼oz) finely crumbled feta cheese and taste for seasoning. Good on griddled chicken or lamb, or roast pumpkin.

MOJO VERDE

A sauce from the Canary Islands that is great on anything griddled: lamb, pork or chicken. Put the leaves from a small bunch each of parsley and coriander and 10g (¼oz) sprigs of mint in a food processor. Add 1 chopped garlic clove, 1 deseeded green chilli, 1½ tsp ground cumin and 3 tbsp red wine vinegar. Blitz, adding 120ml (4fl oz) extra virgin olive oil. Season and taste.

GREEN TAHINI

For lamb and roast veg. Put 100ml (3½fl oz) tahini, 2 tbsp natural yogurt, 2 crushed garlic cloves, juice of 1 lemon, 6 tbsp extra virgin olive oil, 125ml (4fl oz) water and 15g (½oz) parsley or coriander, or a mix, in a food processor. Season. Whizz to a sauce as thick as double cream; you may need more water. Taste for seasoning.

PARSLEY, TOMATO & POMEGRANATE

Deseed and finely chop 135g (5oz) tomatoes. Toss with lots of finely chopped parsley leaves, finely chopped red onion, 1 crushed garlic clove, a squeeze of lemon juice, 4 tbsp extra virgin olive oil and 1 tbsp pomegranate molasses. Good with fish, lamb, or avocado.

MINT, ALMOND & HONEY PESTO

Perfect for lamb or on griddled halloumi cheese. Put 60g (2¼oz) toasted almonds, 3 garlic cloves, 80g (2¾oz) mint leaves, 40g (1½oz) parsley leaves, 3 tsp honey and the juice of 1 lemon into a food processor. Season. Blitz to a purée, adding 300ml (½ pint) extra virgin olive oil in a steady stream.

HAZELNUT PICADA

A Spanish embellishment for roast or griddled pork, lamb or chicken, or roast cauliflower. Fry 30g (1oz) sourdough bread in olive oil until golden. Toast 40g (1½oz) hazelnuts. Crush both in a mortar and pestle with a clove of garlic. Mix in 100ml (3½fl oz) extra virgin olive oil, the grated zest of ½ orange, 1 tbsp sherry vinegar, 1 tbsp sherry and 2 tbsp chopped parsley.

PRESERVED LEMON & RAISIN RELISH

Serve with lamb, tuna and as part of a mezze spread. Crush – in a mortar and pestle, or a food processor using the pulse button – 25g (scant 1oz) blanched almonds, 2 deseeded red chillies, 1 tsp grated root ginger, 2 small garlic cloves and 10g (¼oz) coriander with the juice of ½ lemon, 1 tbsp white balsamic vinegar and 7 tbsp extra virgin olive oil. Stir in the chopped rind of 2 preserved lemons, 45g (1½oz) soaked, drained raisins and seasoning.

ROASTS

poussins with sherry, raisins & pine nuts

I WISH I HAD A POUND for every time I've cooked this. Special enough to serve to friends but totally hassle free. Good with couscous, or little olive oil-roasted potatoes.

SERVES 4
75g (2¾oz) raisins
400ml (14fl oz) medium sherry
4 poussins
olive oil
salt and pepper
25g (scant 1oz) toasted pine nuts (see page 242)

Preheat the oven to 200°C/400°F/gas mark 6.

Put the raisins in a small saucepan with half the sherry and bring to the boil. Remove from the heat and leave to plump up for 30 minutes.

Put the poussins in a roasting tin, or a broad shallow ovenproof dish, in which they will fit quite snugly (if there's a lot of room around them, the juices will evaporate). Drizzle some olive oil over each one and season. Roast for 45 minutes. After 20 minutes, add the remaining sherry.

When there are 15 minutes left before the end of cooking time, add the raisins and the sherry they have soaked in.

After 45 minutes, check for doneness: the birds should still be moist but the juices that run, when pierced between the leg and the rest of the body, should be clear (if there's any trace of pink, cook for a few minutes more, then check again). Serve the poussins in the dish in which they've been cooked, or transfer to a warm serving dish and spoon the cooking juices and raisins around. Scatter with the pine nuts.

roast citrus, ginger & honey chicken

ONE OF MY family's favourite meals (and they're fussy). It's very simple to make but looks pretty spectacular, as the chicken turns dark and glossy because of the honey and the orange wedges become nicely caramelized at the edges. If your chicken is getting too dark as it cooks, cover it with foil.

SERVES 6

For the chicken
1.8kg (4lb) chicken
250ml (9fl oz) orange juice
4 tbsp honey
1½ tbsp hot sauce
3 garlic cloves, grated
2.5cm (1in) root ginger, peeled and grated
finely grated zest of 2 oranges

salt and pepper
200ml (7fl oz) chicken stock or water, if needed

For the roast oranges
4 thin-skinned oranges
olive oil
a little ground ginger
a little soft light brown sugar

Preheat the oven to 190°C/375°F/gas mark 5. Put the chicken into a roasting tin in which it can lie snugly; if it's too big, the cooking juices round the bird will burn. Whisk the rest of the ingredients for the chicken (except the stock or water) in a jug. Pour some of this inside the bird, then pour two-thirds of the rest over it, reserving the remainder. Roast for 45 minutes.

Cut the thin-skinned oranges into wedges and put them into an ovenproof dish where they can lie in a single layer. Sprinkle with olive oil, ground ginger and seasoning and turn them over in this, then sprinkle the sugar on top. Roast alongside the chicken for one hour.

When the chicken has cooked for 45 minutes, take it out of the oven, scoop up the sticky juices around it with a spoon and spread them over the skin. Add the rest of the orange juice mixture to the juices in the tin, stirring well to help them blend, then roast for another 45 minutes. Remove from the oven, put on a warm platter and let the chicken rest for 15 minutes. If the juices seem too thick or intense, add the stock or water to the tin, set it over a high heat and bring to the boil, stirring to dislodge the sticky bits. Serve in a jug. Add the orange wedges to the chicken platter and take it to the table.

roast maple & mustard spatchcock with figs

SPATCHCOCKED CHICKEN – because it's flattened – cooks much more quickly than a whole bird. Supermarkets don't sell them prepared this way, but your butcher will (though it's not hard to do it yourself, as below). Figs, maple and mustard make a lovely combination. Serve with a grain – brown rice, bulgar wheat or freekeh – cooked with finely grated orange zest.

SERVES 4

For the chicken
1.6kg (3lb 8oz) chicken
2 tbsp Dijon mustard
4 tbsp maple syrup
leaves from 6 sprigs of thyme
salt and pepper

For the figs
8 figs, stalks snipped off, halved lengthways
2 tbsp maple syrup
1 tbsp balsamic vinegar

Preheat the oven to 200°C/400°F/gas mark 6.

To spatchcock the chicken, place it breast side down on a chopping board. Using good kitchen scissors, cut through the flesh and bone along both sides of the backbone from the tail end to the head and remove it. Turn the chicken over and press down hard on the breast until you have flattened the chicken. Remove any big globules of fat and neaten any ragged bits of skin.

Mix the mustard, maple syrup and thyme. Put the chicken into a roasting tin and brush this all over it, keeping a little back. Season. Roast the chicken for 45 minutes and, 15 minutes before the end of cooking time, spoon the rest of the maple mixture over the chicken.

When there are 10 minutes before the chicken is ready, put the figs into a small ovenproof dish. Mix the maple syrup and vinegar and spoon this over the cut side of each fig. Season and put into the oven with the chicken. The figs will almost caramelize as they cook.

Cut the chicken into pieces and serve on a warm platter with the glossy figs around it.

yogurt-marinated spatchcock with herbs & pomegranates

A YOGURT OR BUTTERMILK marinade does amazing things to chicken, really tenderizing and flavouring it. If you don't have time to marinate this, make something else!

SERVES 4

For the chicken and marinade
1.6kg (3lb 8oz) chicken
250g (9oz) natural yogurt
   (not Greek yogurt)
juice of ½ lemon
3 tbsp olive oil
4 garlic cloves, crushed
1 tsp cayenne pepper

For the dressing
1 small garlic clove, crushed
salt and pepper
1 red chilli, deseeded and finely chopped
¼ tsp ground cumin

1 tbsp white balsamic vinegar
½ tbsp runny honey
1 tsp pomegranate molasses
1 tbsp lemon juice
4 tbsp extra virgin olive oil

For the salad
60g (2¼oz) soft salad leaves
15g (½oz) sprigs of coriander (remove some of the
   stalks if they are very long)
½ medium red onion, very finely sliced
seeds from ½ pomegranate
2 tbsp roughly chopped pistachio nuts

Spatchcock the chicken (see page 161) or get your butcher to do it. Mix the yogurt, lemon juice, regular olive oil, garlic and cayenne. Put the bird in a dish where it can lie flat. Make small incisions on the underside and lift the skin on the breast. Pour the marinade over and turn to coat. Cover and put in the fridge. Four hours is good, overnight is even better. Turn a few times.

When you're ready to cook, whisk the dressing ingredients together. Taste for seasoning. Return the chicken to room temperature while you preheat the oven to 200°C/400°F/gas mark 6.

Lift the chicken out of its marinade, gently shaking off the excess. Put it in a roasting tin, breast side up, season and roast for 45 minutes. Toss the salad leaves and coriander with the onion and dressing. Scatter with the pomegranate seeds and pistachio nuts and serve the chicken – either whole or cut into pieces – with the salad.

roast spatchcock with chilli & smoky migas

THIS IS A FRIDAY or Saturday night dish, as you do have to keep an eye on the migas. Migas are Spanish: bread pieces soaked in milk, then cooked so they are crispy on the outside and fluffy inside. This dish itself didn't originate anywhere except in my head, but is Spanish-inspired.

SERVES 4

1.6kg (3lb 8oz) chicken
15g (½oz) coriander
15g (½oz) flat leaf parsley
4 garlic cloves, chopped
juice of 2 lemons
125ml (4fl oz) olive oil, plus 2 tbsp
3 red chillies, deseeded and finely sliced

salt and pepper
270g (9¾oz) coarse country bread
4 tbsp milk
½ tsp smoked paprika
1 tbsp balsamic vinegar
1 tbsp dry sherry
125g (4½oz) mixed leaves (I like baby spinach and watercress)

Spatchcock the chicken (see page 161), or get your butcher to do it. Put the herbs, garlic, the juice of 1½ lemons and the 125ml (4fl oz) of olive oil into a food processor. Blend, adding one of the sliced chillies. Put the chicken in a dish where it can lie flat. Make small incisions on the underside. Pour the marinade over, turning to coat. Cover and chill for four hours, if you can. Return to room temperature. Preheat the oven to 200°C/400°F/gas mark 6. Lift the chicken out of the marinade, put into a roasting tin, breast side up, season and roast for 45 minutes.

Tear the bread into pieces about the size of closed mussels. Put in a bowl with the milk and 4 tbsp of water and toss round with your hands. Leave to soak for 30 minutes. Gently squeeze the bread. Heat the remaining 2 tbsp of olive oil in a large frying pan and add the bread. Cook over a medium heat, turning every so often, until dark golden and crisp. Sprinkle on the paprika and season. Cook a little more, turning; it takes 15 minutes in all.

When the chicken is ready, drain off the juices (there won't be many). Mix them with the vinegar and sherry and add the remaining lemon juice, to taste. Taste; it's a dressing to cover everything so shouldn't be exactly like a vinaigrette, nor too oily. Add the remaining chillies.

Put the leaves into a large, broad, shallow serving bowl and put the chicken, cut into pieces, on top. Scatter the migas around, then pour the dressing over everything. Serve immediately.

ishita's chicken masala

TWITTER IS A GREAT PLACE for swapping recipes and I like to hear what others are cooking. This is from @foodwithmustard, one of my favourite tweeters. She suggests serving it in quite a British way, with potatoes roasted with chilli and lemon, and carrots roasted with ginger and cardamom. Hungry yet? The marinating is optional; do it if you have time. To be super-quick, use a bought garam masala blend (about 1½ tbsp) for the spiced butter, instead of separate spices.

SERVES 6

For the marinade and chicken
500g (1lb 2oz) natural yogurt
6 fat garlic cloves, crushed
2cm (¾in) root ginger, peeled and grated
½ tbsp chilli powder
1 tsp ground turmeric
salt and pepper
1.8kg (4lb) chicken

For the spiced butter
100g (3½oz) salted butter, slightly soft
1 tbsp ground coriander
½ tbsp ground cumin
1 tsp chilli powder
1 tsp ground cinnamon
1 tsp ground cloves
½ tsp ground turmeric
2–3 fat garlic cloves, crushed
1cm (½in) root ginger, peeled and grated

Mix all the marinade ingredients and slather this over the chicken and into the cavity as well. Leave overnight in the fridge (though two hours is fine, or cook without marinating). Mash the butter with all its other ingredients and 1 tsp freshly ground black pepper. Chill, to firm up.

Remove the chicken from its marinade, wipe off the excess and return to room temperature. Preheat the oven to 200°C/400°F/gas mark 6. Carefully slip your fingers in between the skin and breasts. Loosen the skin over the legs and thighs, too. Spread the butter under the skin down over the legs, thighs and breasts. Spread the remaining butter on top and sprinkle with salt.

Cook the chicken for one hour 10 minutes, basting every so often. Check to see that it's cooked: the juices that run when pierced between leg and bird should be clear, with no trace of pink. Cover with a double layer of foil and leave to rest for 15 minutes, before serving with the juices.

easy like sunday morning

As a teenager I hated Sunday lunch. My parents usually called on friends at midday, leaving me to cook the vegetables (the meat – an excellent bit of Irish beef – was already in the oven). I was a good cook, but there was something about the grinding dullness of this task, and the fact that I tried to combine it with homework, that made me wilfully incapable of pulling it off. Sunday after Sunday I would let the carrots boil dry, then try to get rid of the smell while prising the burnt batons off the saucepan.

When I was an au pair in France, I went to a Sunday lunch that made me feel as though I was appearing in a Truffaut film. 'That's the way to do it,' I thought. My host Agnes lived with her husband and children in a dilapidated farmhouse. The Sunday lunch in question wasn't grand, but the whole thing was pulled off with style and grace. We drank chilled Pineau de Charente and picked at good charcuterie, then sat down at a table dressed with a simple white cloth and ate roast lamb with petits pois à la française and artichoke hearts (I remember my shock at the absence of potatoes). Afterwards there was a green salad – using just one kind of leaf – with a good dressing; one perfect cheese; and poached peaches. What was special about this meal is that it was unremarkable. There was no endless procession of vegetables and desserts, no complicated dishes. It was chic in its simplicity; served on platters and in big serving bowls, it felt generous and inclusive.

It took me years to approach anything like the ideal that Agnes's lunch had set in my imagination. I loved the idea of a laid-back Sunday lunch, but would always make too many dishes or serve enough desserts to put on a small trolley. When I asked my partner's parents to Sunday lunch for the first time, I actually managed to singe my hair while juggling too many pans. I was able to snip the burnt bit off, but the smell rather gave me away…

I don't like rules – I always want to break them – but here are some guidelines for a relaxed Sunday lunch: no starter, you're not running a restaurant. Charcuterie, olives and radishes are as far as you should go. Have ice, decent gin or some other aperitif, but remember you're not kitting out a bar. Offer no more than two side dishes (one should be easy to make). One pudding is enough. (Though that's hard advice to follow. I always have a fruit pudding – my favourite – and somehow Sunday lunch is a great place for some old-fashioned stodge such as bread-and-butter pudding.) If you can't be bothered to make pudding at all, a bottle of dessert wine is fine, as is cheese, though one big, good cheese is better than four average wedges.

It's difficult to resist the temptation to offer lots of choice, after all it seems generous. But with Sunday lunch, as with so many things, less is more. Keep it simple.

honeyed pork loin with plum & lavender relish

I COOK THIS A LOT, using different accompaniments depending on the time of year. You can make the relish with fresh apricots or, in the autumn, use pears or apples with rosemary. It's fabulous with pickled peaches, too. The pork is still ever-so-slightly pink in the middle when cooked at this temperature and for this length of time, so cook it a little longer if you want to… but most people overcook pork, so be careful.

SERVES 8

For the relish
650g (1lb 7oz) plums, halved and pitted
½ onion, roughly chopped
pinch of chilli flakes
2cm (¾in) root ginger, peeled and grated
100g (3½oz) soft light brown sugar, or to taste
2 tbsp red wine vinegar
juice of ½ lemon
salt and pepper
2 sprigs of fresh lavender

For the pork
2kg (4lb 8oz) loin of pork, off the bone (get the butcher to remove the skin and leave about 1cm/½in of fat on the joint)
leaves from 2 sprigs of rosemary, chopped
2 tbsp Dijon mustard
3½ tbsp runny honey
juice of ½ lemon

Put all the ingredients for the relish, except the lavender, in a heavy-based pan. Bring to the boil, stirring, then reduce the heat. Simmer for 35 minutes, stirring every so often. Once the plums start to fall apart, add the lavender. Taste for balance; you might need more sugar. Leave to cool.

Make incisions all over the flesh side of the pork and stuff in the rosemary. Season. Mix the mustard, honey and lemon juice, pour about three-quarters over and into the incisions. Cover and put in the fridge to marinate for a few hours. Return to room temperature before cooking.

Preheat the oven to 220°C/425°F/gas mark 7. Roll the loin and tie it at intervals with kitchen string. Put into a roasting tin fat side up, pouring over the marinade from the fridge. Cook for 15 minutes, then reduce the oven temperature to 180°C/350°F/gas mark 4 and cook for one hour, basting every so often. Add the reserved honey mix 10 minutes before the end of cooking. If it gets too dark, cover with foil. Check it is cooked: the juices should run clear when pierced. Cover with foil, insulate (use tea towels) and rest for 15 minutes. Serve hot or warm, with the relish.

spanish spiced pork with sherried onions

I LIKE THE WAY THAT CUMIN – probably my favourite spice – is used in Spanish food. It's part of the Arab legacy and works surprisingly well with sherry, lending an earthy base note to the sweetness.

SERVES 6

3 garlic cloves, crushed
½ tbsp ground cumin
3 tsp paprika
sea salt flakes and pepper
5 sprigs of thyme
5 tbsp extra virgin olive oil
1.5kg (3lb 5oz) boned, rolled free-range pork
   loin, skin off, but a layer of fat left on

5 small red onions, cut into slim crescent
   moon-shaped slices
15g (½oz) unsalted butter
2 bay leaves
300ml (½ pint) sweet oloroso or cream sherry
50ml (2fl oz) sherry vinegar

Mix the garlic, cumin, paprika, salt, pepper, leaves from three sprigs of thyme and the oil. Open the loin so the meaty bit is facing you and make incisions all over it. Spread the spice mixture over it and into the incisions. Cover with cling film and marinate for a few hours in the fridge.

When you're ready to cook, preheat the oven to 150°C/300°F/gas mark 2 and return the meat to room temperature. Roll the pork and tie it at intervals with kitchen string. Heat an ovenproof pan or casserole dish with a lid that will fit the pork. Brown the pork all over – the oil from the marinade will be enough – then remove it. Sauté the onions in the oil in the pan until beginning to soften, then add the butter (for flavour), reduce the heat and cook for four minutes. Add the rest of the thyme, the bay, sherry and vinegar. Bring to the boil, then reduce the heat. Return the pork and put the lid on. Cook in the oven for one hour 30 minutes, or until cooked but not dry, turning the joint from time to time and basting with its liquid. Remove the pork to a warm dish and let it rest for 10 minutes, covered loosely with foil.

Boil the onion mixture until it has thickened a bit. Taste and adjust the seasoning if you need to. Serve the pork with the onions, little olive oil-roasted potatoes and spinach.

slow-cooked pork with chipotle tomato sauce

OK, NOT ONE FOR a Wednesday night. In fact I know that cooking anything for 10 hours might seem like a hassle, but trust me, this couldn't be less demanding. Get it going on a Saturday morning, then serve to friends for a laid-back Saturday supper. It's lovely with hot sweet potatoes (see page 186). If you can't find chipotle chillies in adobo (it comes in cans), just use chipotle chillies soaked in hot water, or chipotle paste. Chipotle is what gives the smoky flavour.

SERVES ABOUT 10

For the pork
4kg (9lb) pork shoulder on the bone,
    skin removed
6 tbsp Dijon mustard
2½ tbsp soft light brown sugar
¾ tbsp sea salt flakes
1 tbsp paprika

For the sauce
2 tbsp olive oil
2 onions, finely chopped
6 garlic cloves, chopped
2 tbsp chipotle chillies in adobo sauce
2 x 400g cans of cherry tomatoes in thick juice
1½ tbsp soft dark brown sugar
salt and pepper

Preheat the oven to 110°C/225°F/gas mark ¼.

If the meat seems a bit wet, dry it with kitchen paper. Spread the mustard over the fat. Mix together the sugar, salt and paprika and pat that on to the mustard. Set fat side up on a rack in a roasting tin and cook for 10 hours, basting the exposed meat every so often during that time. It will become really soft.

To make the sauce, heat the oil in a pan and sauté the onions until soft (about 12 minutes), then add the garlic and cook for another couple of minutes. Add the chipotles, tomatoes, sugar and seasoning and bring to the boil. Reduce the heat to low and cook uncovered for 20–30 minutes, stirring every so often. You should have a thick sauce, but make sure it doesn't taste too intense and add a little water if you've cooked it too far. Serve the pork with the sauce.

pork loin with pumpkin purée & pecorino

THIS IS A DODDLE, and looks very impressive. Get your butcher to remove the skin from the pork and leave about 1cm (½in) of fat. The purée can be made earlier in the day and gently reheated to serve.

SERVES 8

For the pork
2kg (4lb 8oz) boneless pork loin, skin off
6 garlic cloves, sliced
3 tsp fennel seeds
1 tsp chilli flakes
4 tbsp olive oil
salt and pepper

For the purée
1.2kg (2lb 10oz) butternut squash or
   well-flavoured pumpkin
olive oil
freshly grated nutmeg
100g (3½oz) mascarpone
pecorino cheese, shaved, to serve

Lay the pork on a board, flesh side up, and make incisions all over it with a sharp knife. Push slivers of garlic into the incisions. Crush the fennel and chilli in a mortar and pestle, add the olive oil, season and rub this all over the flesh, pushing bits down inside the slits. Put in a dish, cover and put in the fridge overnight, then return it to room temperature before cooking.

Preheat the oven to 220°C/425°F/gas mark 7. Roll the loin and tie at intervals with kitchen string (not too tight; it should hold its shape, not look like a sausage). Cook for 25 minutes. Reduce the oven temperature to 180°C/350°F/gas mark 4 and cook for one hour, basting now and then. Cut the squash into wedges and remove the seeds. Put the wedges into a roasting tin, drizzle with olive oil, season and bake alongside the pork until completely tender, about 40 minutes.

Check the pork for doneness; the juices should run clear with no trace of pink when pierced. Cover with foil, insulate (I use tea towels) and allow to rest for 15 minutes.

Discard the skin from the squash. Purée with plenty of seasoning, nutmeg and the mascarpone. Gently heat, then scrape into a warm dish and top with pecorino shavings. Serve with the pork.

balinese roast pork

BASED ON A DISH CALLED *babi guling,* where a whole pig is cooked
with the spice paste. A good, simple, different Sunday lunch.

SERVES 6–8

For the spice paste
2 lemongrass stalks
3 kaffir lime leaves
1 tbsp ground turmeric
3 shallots (1 if they're long), chopped
3 red or green chillies, deseeded, chopped
3 garlic cloves, chopped
small handful of coriander leaves
15g (½oz) root ginger, peeled and grated
2 tbsp coriander seeds, crushed
1 tbsp black peppercorns, ground
1 tbsp palm sugar, or soft light brown sugar
juice of 1 lime
2 tbsp flavourless oil, such as groundnut

For the pork
1.8kg (4lb) pork belly
1 tbsp ground turmeric
2 tbsp flavourless oil, such as groundnut
sea salt flakes

Take the coarse outer leaves off the lemongrass, then chop the white bit (discard the rest). Put
everything for the spice paste into a food processor and blitz to form a purée. Score the pork
skin, marking it in parallel lines. Turn the pork over and make big gashes all over the flesh to
create small pockets. Rub the paste over this (not on the skin), pushing it into the pockets, put
in a dish, cover with cling film and allow to marinate in the fridge for a few hours.

When you're ready to cook, preheat the oven to 220°C/425°F/gas mark 7. Roll the pork up and
tie it at intervals with kitchen string. Place on a rack in roasting tin, with the join underneath.
Mix the turmeric and oil together and rub this all over, then sprinkle with salt flakes. Roast
for 15 minutes. Reduce the oven temperature to 160°C/325°F/gas mark 3 and cook for another
one hour and 15 minutes, basting occasionally with the juices. Rest, covered with foil, for
10–15 minutes. Remove the string and serve with rice and stir-fried greens. South-east Asian
fruit salad with chilli & tamarind (see page 41) is great on the side.

slow-cooked lamb with pomegranates & honey

EASY, BUT RICH AND EXOTIC, a real feast for a long lazy weekend lunch or dinner. The lamb should be very soft, almost falling apart, but cooking time varies depending on the time of year, so start checking it after four hours.

SERVES 6

For the lamb
2kg (4lb 8oz) bone-in shoulder of lamb
9 garlic cloves, roughly chopped
sea salt flakes and pepper
leaves from a small bunch of mint, torn
4½ tbsp pomegranate molasses
4½ tbsp runny honey
4 tbsp olive oil
juice from 4 lemons

To serve
1 pomegranate, or 225g (8oz)
    pomegranate seeds
leaves from a small bunch of mint, torn
4 garlic cloves, crushed
400g (14oz) Greek yogurt
flatbreads or couscous
salad of watercress or spinach,
    coarse stalks removed

Pierce the lamb all over deeply. Crush the garlic to a paste with salt – it acts as an abrasive – in a mortar. Add the other ingredients for the lamb, starting with the mint, and pound some more.

Put the meat on two huge pieces of foil set at right angles in a roasting tin and pull up the sides so none of the marinade will run out. Pour on the marinade, turning the lamb. Cover and put in the fridge for about 12 hours.

Return the meat to room temperature and preheat the oven to 200°C/400°F/gas mark 6. Pull the foil over the lamb and seal to form a tent. Place in the oven and immediately reduce the oven temperature to 160°C/325°F/gas mark 3. Cook for four to five hours, basting with the juices every so often. The lamb is cooked when you can pull the meat apart with a fork. (Cooking times vary a lot depending on the age of the meat you are using, so start checking after four hours.)

Mix the pomegranate seeds with the mint, then add the garlic to the yogurt. Shred the lamb at the table and serve with the yogurt, pomegranate and mint, plus flatbreads or couscous and a salad of watercress and spinach (a green salad tossed with walnuts or hazelnuts would be great).

roast lamb loin fillets with zhoggiu

A MINI ROAST – using lamb loin fillets – just for two and with a Sicilian sauce. Be careful not to overcook the meat. Sautéed potatoes are perfect on the side.

SERVES 2

For the sauce
25g (scant 1oz) blanched almonds, toasted
pinch of sea salt flakes and pepper
1 garlic clove, roughly chopped
10g (¼oz) flat leaf parsley leaves
10g (¼oz) mint leaves
1 tbsp white balsamic vinegar
2½ tbsp extra virgin olive oil
squeeze of lemon juice

For the lamb
2 lamb loin fillets, trimmed
1 tbsp olive oil

Make the sauce first so that it's all ready, but don't do it more than 30 minutes in advance: the fresher the better. Crush the nuts roughly in a mortar and pestle. Add the salt and the garlic and continue to crush until the garlic has broken down. Add the herbs – in two batches as it makes it easier to deal with – and pound hard until you have something like a rough purée. While still pounding, add the vinegar and then a little of the extra virgin olive oil at a time. Add lemon juice to taste – sometimes just a spritz is enough – and check the seasoning.

Preheat the oven to 200°C/400°F/gas mark 6.

Sprinkle the lamb with salt and pepper and heat the regular olive oil in a frying pan over a high heat. Brown the lamb all over to get a good colour, then transfer to a roasting tin. Season with salt and roast for 10 minutes. Cover and keep warm while the meat rests for 10 minutes.

Cut the lamb into neat slices and serve on warm plates. Spoon the sauce alongside and serve, with sprigs of watercress, if you like.

indian roast leg of lamb

MY VERSION OF A FAMOUS DISH from Lucknow. The marinating is important in this recipe – it really affects the flavour and texture of the lamb – so leave it for a whole day if you can. Serve it with rice and chutneys, or with Indian-spiced roast root vegetables for an Anglo-Indian Sunday lunch.

SERVES 8

100g (3½oz) desiccated coconut

3 tbsp vegetable oil

2 onions, finely sliced

30g (1oz) root ginger, peeled and finely grated

6 garlic cloves, crushed

seeds from 6 green and 6 black cardamom
    pods, ground

2 tsp chilli powder

2 tbsp garam masala

55g (2oz) cashew nuts

salt and pepper

350g (12oz) natural yogurt (not Greek yogurt)

juice of 1 lemon or 2 limes

2kg (4lb 8oz) leg of lamb

Put the coconut in a bowl and pour over just enough boiling water to cover. Leave to soak for one hour. Meanwhile, heat the oil and fry the onions until they are deep golden brown; it will take quite a while. Add the ginger and garlic and cook for another three minutes or so, then add both types of cardamom and the chilli and cook for another couple of minutes. Drain the coconut. Put the onion mixture into a food processor and add everything else except the lamb. Whizz to a purée.

Take the fat off the lamb and pull off the parchment-like skin, too. Make deep gashes all over the meat. Put it into a roasting tin and pour over the purée, turning and making sure it goes into the gashes. Cover with cling film and marinate in the fridge for 24 hours.

When you're ready to cook, preheat the oven to 200°C/400°F/gas mark 6. Let the lamb return to room temperature, then cover it with foil and cook for 20 minutes. Reduce the oven temperature to 180°C/350°F/gas mark 4 and cook for a further 50 minutes, removing the foil for the last 30 minutes so it browns. Cover the lamb with a double layer of foil and allow it to rest for 15–20 minutes before serving, with chutneys and yogurt.

roast lamb with peas, onions & vermouth

A ROAST WHERE nearly everything can be cooked in the same dish.
Bliss. All you need to add are some little potatoes and maybe roast
peppers or artichoke hearts tossed with lemon juice and chopped
parsley leaves.

SERVES 8
2kg (4lb 8oz) leg of lamb
3 garlic cloves, cut into slivers
salt and pepper
extra virgin olive oil
300ml (½ pint) dry vermouth
8 small onions, cut into wedges
10 anchovies, drained of oil and chopped
600g (1lb 5oz) frozen peas, or fresh peas when in season
leaves from 8 sprigs of mint, roughly torn

Preheat the oven to 220°C/425F/gas mark 7.

Pierce the lamb all over with a small sharp knife to make little incisions. Push all the slivers
of garlic into these. Put into a roasting tin and rub all over with salt, pepper and olive oil. Put
into the hot oven and roast for 20 minutes.

Add half the vermouth and all the onions to the tin. Reduce the oven temperature to
180°C/350°F/gas mark 4. Roast for 15 minutes, basting every so often with the cooking juices.

Pour in the remaining vermouth, add the anchovies and cook for 25 minutes. Stir in the peas
and roast for another 15 minutes. This gives you rosy (but not bloody) lamb.

Move the lamb to a warm platter and leave to rest for 15 minutes. Just before serving reheat the
peas and onions, add the mint and spoon this around the lamb.

lamb with preserved lemon, dates & cumin butter

STUFFED LEG OF LAMB is easy, as long as you have someone around to help you tie the string round the joint. This isn't a midweek meal, but it's good for friends on a Saturday night, or for Sunday lunch. Serve with couscous, rice or bulgar wheat. The stuffing and cayenne butter provide enough interest, but a bowl of garlic-scented yogurt would be good on the side (plus maybe an easy vegetable dish).

SERVES 8

For the lamb
175g (6oz) kale, coarse stalks removed
15g (½oz) unsalted butter
1 red chilli, deseeded and chopped
½ tsp ground cumin
salt and pepper
5 dates, pitted and chopped
2 preserved lemons, flesh removed, rind chopped
2kg (4lb 8oz) boned leg of lamb

For the butter
50g (1¾oz) unsalted butter, softened
1 tsp ground cumin
1 tsp cayenne pepper
3 garlic cloves, grated

Preheat the oven to 220°C/425°F/gas mark 7. Cook the kale in boiling water for five minutes, then drain and run cold water through it. Squeeze out as much moisture as you can. Chop roughly.

Melt the butter in a frying pan and sauté the kale in this, with the chilli, for a couple of minutes. Add the cumin and cook for another minute. Season and add the dates and preserved lemons.

Lay the lamb on a board, fat side down, and season. Put the stuffing in the centre, then fold the meat over, pressing lightly to seal. Tie at intervals with kitchen string to keep it in shape. Make deep incisions all over with a sharp knife and put it in a roasting tin. Mix all the ingredients for the butter, push into the incisions and rub all over the outside. Roast, with the join underneath, for 20 minutes. Reduce the oven temperature to 180°C/350°F/gas mark 4 and cook for one hour. Cover with a double layer of foil and rest for 15–20 minutes. Serve with the cooking juices.

CHOPS &
SAUSAGES

coffee-brined pork chops with hot sweet potatoes

THIS SOUNDS STRANGE, but it works. The coffee gives the chops
a good deep flavour, almost tobacco-ey. Them Southern cooks know
a thing or two about pork.

SERVES 4

6 tbsp soft dark brown or molasses sugar

30g (1oz) sea salt flakes

1 litre (1¾ pints) freshly brewed hot coffee

4 big pork chops, 250–275g (9–9¾oz) each

4 sweet potatoes

pepper

1½ tbsp rendered pork fat, lard, or flavourless oil

25g (scant 1oz) unsalted butter

leaves from 4 sprigs of thyme

1 red and 1 green chilli, deseeded and finely sliced

Stir the sugar and salt flakes into the coffee until dissolved. Add 200ml (7fl oz) of cold water and leave to cool completely. Put this brine in a large container and add the chops, making sure they're submerged. Cover and put in the fridge for six to eight hours.

Remove the chops from the marinade and pat dry with kitchen paper. Return the chops to the fridge – uncovered, so they dry out a little – and leave for a couple more hours.

When you're ready to eat, preheat the oven to 200°C/400°F/gas mark 6. Bake the sweet potatoes for about 30 minutes, timing them to be ready at the same time as the chops.

Season the chops (you won't need much salt, but pepper is important), heat the fat or oil in a frying pan and cook over a high heat on both sides and on the fat to get a good colour. Reduce the heat to medium and continue, turning every so often, until cooked (eight to 10 minutes).

Melt the butter in a small frying pan and add the thyme and chillies. Cook for about a minute, then split the sweet potatoes and drizzle the insides with the butter. Serve with the chops.

pork chops with mustard & capers

A CLASSIC, but none the worse for that. I love the way the richness of the cream is cut by the capers.

SERVES 4

1 tbsp olive oil

salt and pepper

4 pork chops, 225–250g (8–9oz) each

275ml (9½fl oz) dry vermouth

250g (9oz) double cream

1½ tsp Dijon mustard

2 tbsp capers, well rinsed of salt or brine

Preheat the oven to 200°C/400°F/gas mark 6.

Heat the oil in a large ovenproof frying pan (or two smaller pans) over a high heat. Season the chops all over and cook them for two minutes on each side; you want them good and golden. Now brown the fat, too. Transfer the pan to the oven and cook for 12 minutes.

Wearing good oven gloves and being careful of the hot pan handle, pour the fat out of the pan; put the chops on a warm plate and cover to keep warm. Add the vermouth to the pan. Bring to the boil and reduce by half, stirring to pick up all the browned savoury bits on the pan, then pour in the cream. Boil until the sauce coats the back of a spoon. Take it off the heat, whisk in the mustard and add the capers. Taste: it's a strong sauce but it works well with the pork.

Serve the chops with the sauce spooned over the top.

pork chops with figs & marsala

A VERY GOOD SUPPER for two or even four (double the quantities and use two pans). Some people – even Italians – will tell you that dry Marsala doesn't exist. It does. You might have a bit of trouble tracking it down but it's a really useful booze to have around, rich and raisiny. You could also use a medium sherry, if you can't find Marsala.

SERVES 2
30g (1oz) unsalted butter, chilled
2 tsp olive oil
5 fat ripe figs, stalks snipped off, halved lengthways
salt and pepper
2 x 225g (8oz) pork chops, off the bone
200ml (7fl oz) dry Marsala
200ml (7fl oz) well-flavoured chicken stock

Heat 10g (¼oz) of the butter and all the oil in a frying pan. Add the figs and cook briefly over a high heat on the cut sides, so they get nice and golden. Remove from the pan and set aside.

Season the chops on both sides and quickly brown them in the fat in the pan over a medium-high heat. Cook them on both sides and then brown the fat, too. Reduce the heat and continue to cook, turning frequently, until cooked through. Take them out of the pan, set aside and cover to keep warm.

Pour the fat out of the pan, but don't wipe or wash it. Add the Marsala and bring to the boil, scraping the bottom of the pan. Reduce by about half, then add the stock and reduce that, too, until you are left with enough to make a sauce for two people.

Return the figs to the pan to heat through and soften the uncut sides, then push them to the side and add the rest of the butter. Swirl it around, whisking it into the Marsala and stock. It should make the juices glossy. Serve the chops immediately with the figs and Marsala sauce.

lamb chops with walnut, chilli & honey salsa verde

I SEEM TO HAVE GOT INTO pounding things during the last few years. I like highly flavoured mixtures such as this salsa verde where the components combine, but keep their identity and texture. This salsa – sweet, sour and hot – is also good with roast aubergines, even potatoes.

SERVES 4
1 fat garlic clove, chopped
sea salt flakes and pepper
2 green chillies, deseeded and chopped
leaves from a small bunch of mint
50g (1¾oz) walnuts
1 tbsp capers, rinsed and roughly chopped
3 tsp honey
juice of ½ lemon
8 tbsp extra virgin olive oil
8 lamb loin chops
olive oil

Grind the garlic and a pinch of salt to a paste in a mortar; the salt helps as it acts as an abrasive. Add the chillies and mint and pound until you have a rough mixture. Add the walnuts and pound until you have a coarse purée. Tip in the capers and pound a bit more. Stir in the honey, lemon juice, extra virgin olive oil and some pepper. Taste to check the sweet-savoury balance.

You can fry the chops or cook them on a ridged griddle pan. If you're using a frying pan, heat a couple of tbsp of regular olive oil in the pan. If you're griddling, heat the griddle until really hot and brush the chops with regular olive oil. Either way, season the chops and put them in the pan or on the griddle. Cook over a high heat until browned on both sides and on the fat, then reduce the heat and cook for a further three minutes each side for chops that are pink and tender in the middle.

Serve the chops with the sauce.

lamb cutlets with cider, mint & cream

A GREAT OLD-FASHIONED DISH from Normandy. Lovely in summer (drink it with rosé or cold cider), but in the autumn you can make the same sauce using sprigs of thyme or rosemary (don't use too much, as rosemary is strong) and serve it with either chops or a roast leg of lamb.

SERVES 6

15g (½oz) unsalted butter
2 shallots, very finely chopped
generous slug of Calvados or brandy
150ml (5fl oz) dry cider
leaves from 5 sprigs of mint
350ml (12fl oz) well-flavoured lamb stock, or chicken stock will do
salt and pepper
18 best end lamb cutlets, well cleaned (ask your butcher to do that)
200ml (7fl oz) double cream

Get the sauce ready so you can just finish it off when the cutlets are done. Melt the butter in a saucepan and sauté the shallots over a medium heat until soft but not coloured. Add the Calvados and let it bubble away until there are only a couple of tbsp left, then add the cider with the mint from three of the sprigs and bring to the boil. Boil until reduced by two-thirds. Take off the heat and leave to infuse for 30 minutes, then strain and mix with the stock. Return to the boil, then reduce by half. Stir in the cream, season and bring to the boil. Boil until you have a sauce that just coats the back of a spoon. Set aside.

Heat a griddle pan. Season the meat well. When the pan is really hot, cook the cutlets on each side until well-coloured, pressing the meaty parts down on the griddle as you're cooking. They should still be pink in the middle, so about a minute and a half on each side should do. Check to see how the cutlets are doing by inserting a sharp knife into one of them.

Quickly reheat the sauce, add the rest of the mint leaves, torn, and check the seasoning. Serve the cutlets on a platter with the sauce and green beans or a watercress salad.

194

lamb chops with fennel & parsley-anchovy relish

OKAY, THIS HAS THREE ELEMENTS – the chops, relish and vegetables
– but each is quick to put together. Use whatever kind of chops you
want (cutlets, chump...) and, another time, try the relish and vegetables
with baked bream, red mullet or sea bass instead.

SERVES 6

For the chops and vegetables
2 small fennel bulbs
juice of ½ lemon
400g (14oz) waxy potatoes (no need to peel)
extra virgin olive oil
salt and pepper
12 plum tomatoes, sliced 5mm (¼in) thick
12 lamb loin chops, or cutlets

For the relish
50g can of cured anchovies, drained of oil and chopped
2½ tbsp chopped flat leaf parsley leaves
6 tbsp extra virgin olive oil
juice of ½ lemon

Preheat the oven to 190°C/375°F/gas mark 5. Quarter the fennel bulbs. Remove the thick outer layer, trim the tops and the bases and remove the cores. Keep any little fronds. Slice really finely. Put it in a large shallow ovenproof dish (I use cast iron, 30cm/12in across) and toss in the lemon juice. Cut the potatoes in slices as thick as a 50p coin and toss them with the fennel, 2½ tbsp of olive oil and seasoning. Lay the tomatoes on top, season and drizzle with a little more oil. Bake for 45 minutes, or until you can feel that the potatoes are tender.

To make the relish, just mix the ingredients together, seasoning generously with pepper.

When there are just eight minutes before the vegetables are ready, brush the chops with olive oil and season. Cook them in a very hot frying or griddle pan: start on a high heat to get a good colour (and brown the fat, too), then reduce the heat and cook until done the way you like them; I like them rare. Serve with the vegetables and relish.

CHOPS & SAUSAGES

chops away

IN THE CAR on the way home from school we knew it was a bad day when mum said, rather grimly, 'What do you lot want for your tea?' Murmurings of 'Dunno' would be followed by the inevitable: 'Do you want pork chops?' My siblings and I would exchange oh-God-no glances.

My mum is a really good cook, but pork chops were the dreaded meal, not because of mum's cooking, but because they were so boring. It's not that a quality chop – a slab of juicy meat and a bone to chew on – can't make a supremely satisfying supper, it's just that they're one of those basics we turn to when we can't think of anything else. More often than not they end up, unseasoned, under a lukewarm grill, their only hope of flavour coming from the jar of mustard on the table beside them.

And finding good pork chops isn't easy. Most of us shop in supermarkets for at least some of our food, but you won't find a decent pork chop in any of them. It doesn't matter that they're free-range or that you cook them with the utmost care, if you want good pork chops, go to a really good butcher (or a farm shop or a farmer's market) and buy chops that have been taken from a rare-breed pig. They won't be cheap, but they're the only pork chops worth bothering with. The meat will be succulent, sweet, even slightly gamey. If you can't afford them, eat something else and have pork chops as a once-in-a-while-treat.

Small chops come from the foreloin and are sometimes called pork cutlets, then there's middle loin chops and – the most generous – chump chops (these don't have a bone). I start chops off in a frying pan over a high heat to get a good colour on each side (I also cook the fat by propping the chops up on their sides), then reduce the heat and cook them through, about another four minutes on each side.

As most lamb isn't (yet) intensively farmed, it's a less problematic choice. There are neat little cutlets from the rack, loin chops, which are meatier, then chump chops, which are really generous and come from the area where the leg meets the loin. Lamb chops are a quick option: the meat should be pink so, unlike with pork, you don't have to worry about cooking it all the way through. Some of the best lamb chop meals are incredibly simple, too. I remember the first time I had lamb *scottadito* ('burn your fingers' lamb) in a restaurant in Italy. Tiny lamb cutlets, marinated in olive oil, rosemary and chilli, then griddled with care, arrived on a big platter and we just ate them with our hands. I still think about this dish, 25 years later, which says something.

Have a look at the spread on sauces and relishes (see pages 152–153) to find ideas for both lamb and pork. Chops aren't a cheap option, so they need to be treated with respect. They should never be the dull fallback… and they needn't be.

oregano lamb chops with greek htipiti

SERVE THESE MARINATED CHOPS simply with yogurt, if you prefer (or yogurt with spicy butter poured over, see page 260), or add a little chilli to the htipiti if you like a bit of heat.

SERVES 6

For the marinade and chops
3 garlic cloves, crushed
1 tbsp dried oregano
100ml (3½ fl oz) olive oil
juice of 2 lemons, plus lemon wedges to serve
salt and pepper
12 lamb loin chops, or cutlets

For the htipiti
1 small red onion, quartered
4 red peppers, halved and deseeded
3 tbsp extra virgin olive oil
1 small garlic clove, crushed
150g (5½oz) feta cheese, finely crumbled
2 tbsp lemon juice, or to taste

Mix everything for the chops in a large bowl, seasoning well, and add the chops. Turn them over in the flavoured oil, cover with cling film and leave to marinate in the fridge for a few hours.

When you're ready to cook, return the lamb to room temperature and preheat the oven to 200°C/400°F/gas mark 6. Brush the onion and peppers with a little of the extra virgin olive oil, put them in a roasting tin, season and roast for 30 minutes, or until completely soft. Either chop them by hand, or blitz very coarsely in a food processor (use the pulse button or you'll end up with a purée), adding the garlic. Stir in the crumbled feta cheese, remaining extra virgin olive oil and lemon juice, then mash it together and check the seasoning.

Preheat a ridged griddle pan until it's really hot. Cook the chops for a couple of minutes on each side – and on the fat, too, to get some colour – until they are done to your liking (loin chops take longer). Transfer to a platter and serve with lemon wedges and the htipiti.

spiced lamb cutlets with dates, feta, sumac & tahini

I CANNOT RESIST the combination of lamb, sweet dates and nutty tahini. You need plenty of herbs, though, to cut through the sweetness here, so use loads and don't stint on the feta cheese either. Greek yogurt and shreds of preserved lemon zest would help, too. Serve with couscous, bulgar wheat or little olive oil-roasted potatoes.

SERVES 4

8 lamb cutlets
5 tbsp olive oil
2 tsp ground cumin
3 garlic cloves, crushed
1½ tsp Aleppo pepper, or 1 tsp cayenne
juice of 1 lemon
50ml (2fl oz) plus 2 tbsp extra virgin olive oil
50g (2oz) tahini
4 tbsp Greek yogurt

salt and pepper
10 fat, soft dates, pitted and quartered
100g (3½oz) barrel-aged feta cheese, crumbled
leaves from a big bunch of mint, torn if large
fronds from a bunch of dill, very roughly chopped
baby leaves or micro leaves (whatever you can find)
1 tbsp white balsamic vinegar
¼ tsp sumac

Put the lamb in a shallow container with the regular olive oil, cumin, two of the garlic cloves, the Aleppo pepper and half the lemon juice. Turn, cover and chill for 30 minutes to two hours.

Tip the remaining garlic and lemon juice, the 50ml (2fl oz) of extra virgin olive oil, tahini, yogurt and seasoning into a blender, pour in 50ml (2fl oz) of water and whizz. It should be the consistency of thick double cream, so add more water if you need to, then check the seasoning.

Heat a griddle or frying pan until really hot. Lift the cutlets out of the marinade, shaking off excess, and cook over a high heat, seasoning as you do, until as you like them (I like them rare).

Put the dates, feta cheese, herbs and leaves on to a platter and toss with seasoning, the vinegar and the 2 tbsp of extra virgin olive oil. Put the cutlets on top, drizzle on some of the dressing (serve the rest on the side) and sprinkle on the sumac. Serve immediately.

honeyed sausages with blackberry & caraway slaw

GOOD-QUALITY SAUSAGES are vital here. The slaw is still lovely without blackberries, but cultivated berries are easy to buy in the autumn, so you don't have to pick your own.

SERVES 4

For the sausages
2 tbsp wholegrain mustard
6 tbsp honey
salt and pepper
8 good-quality chunky pork sausages

For the slaw
1½ tsp caraway seeds
1½ tbsp maple syrup
1 tsp Dijon mustard

1½ tbsp cider vinegar
6 tbsp extra virgin olive oil
75g (2¾oz) baby spinach leaves
¼ small red cabbage, core removed, very finely sliced
1 small apple, cored and cut into matchsticks
¼ small red onion, sliced wafer thin
15g (½oz) walnut pieces, toasted (see page 112)
1 crumbled dried chilli
75g (2¾oz) blackberries

Preheat the oven to 210°C/410°F/gas mark 6½.

Mix the wholegrain mustard and honey with some seasoning. Put the sausages into a roasting tin large enough for there to be a little room around them (too big a tin and the juices will boil off and burn; too small and the sausages will sit in a pool of liquid and won't turn lovely and glossy). Pour the honey mixture over the sausages to coat, then roast for 25–30 minutes, turning every so often. They should look as shiny and dark as conkers. If not, cook for a little longer.

Toast the caraway seeds in a dry frying pan for 20 seconds, then put on to a plate to cool. Whisk together the maple syrup, Dijon mustard, vinegar and extra virgin olive oil and add the seeds.

Bunch the spinach leaves on a chopping board and slice them finely. Put into a serving bowl with the other slaw ingredients, pour on the dressing and gently toss. Serve with the sausages.

simply sausages

PRETTY MUCH EVERYONE loves a sausage. The fact that we often eat them when having a good time – hot dogs at music festivals, barbies on the beach, Bonfire Night – means they come with the happiest associations, too. Give me the most average porker in a roll with fried onions and mustard and I'll want to kick my shoes off and turn the music up *loud*. When I lived in France for a year, I felt sorry for them. Despite the fact that they have great charcuterie, hot dogs were, apparently, beyond their imagination. (This situation has changed, at least in Paris, where American food trucks have introduced *chiens chauds* served in mini baguettes. Oooh la la.)

We have been told to watch our consumption of sausages – the nitrites and nitrates that go into them (as well as into bacon, ham and salamis) – are not good for you, but I won't be giving them up (I eat them every couple of months). All the more reason that, when you *do* have sausages, you make something good with them.

Not so long ago, sausages were just a cheap and cheerful British supper. There wasn't a lot of choice, only pork (fleshy pink and rather unappetizing under plastic wrap) served with mash or, once we started to take them more seriously, onion gravy; in the mid-1990s every gastropub worth its blackboard menu was swimming in onion gravy. Chefs feverishly cooked links of meaty Cumberlands and food markets began to boast speciality sausage stalls. This enthusiasm has continued and broadened. Spanish chorizo – the cured Spanish sausage spiced with paprika – is so popular you'd think we all had an aunt hidden away in Andalucia… though, despite our ardour, we still can't pronounce it: it's chor-*eetho*, amigos, not chor-*itso*. It ain't Italian.

Buying really good (and thus more expensive) sausages less often has made me appreciate them more. While we now cast our net wider in terms of types of sausage, I'll bet you can't think of much to do with them. Don't get me wrong: there's nothing the matter with a plate of sausages and fried eggs. But sausages make fine stews, gorgeous smoky braises when paired with beans or lentils. Or brown sausages, then cook them in stock with waxy potatoes, black pudding and onions to make a pot of soothing Dublin Coddle (don't be misled by the simplicity of this, it's really good); or with pears, rosemary, onions and cider. You can go spicy, too, serving hot Italian sausages with braised lentils, or frying them with purple-sprouting broccoli, garlic, red chilli and a splash of dry vermouth. Chorizo can be sautéed with red peppers and potatoes, stir-fried with squid and coriander or just eaten in sizzling slices with a glass of cold fino.

There are good accompaniments, too, and I don't just mean stewed apples: plums can be cooked with red wine vinegar, brown sugar and ginger; or make a simple sauce of reduced cream, Dijon mustard and a squeeze of lemon juice. A sausage fry-up? A hot dog? They'll always make me smile. But they're only the beginning…

spanish rice with chorizo, beans & pumpkin

DISHES MADE WITH SPANISH RICE must, unlike risotto, be left alone: you shouldn't stir them, which is a big plus in my opinion. It means they're easy. The only taxing thing here is cutting the pumpkin into chunks and peeling it. Do try and use a dish about the same size as mine, as using something bigger or smaller will affect the cooking time.

SERVES 6

generous pinch of saffron strands (optional)
1½ tbsp olive oil
10–12 chorizo sausages (the type that need cooking, not the cured version)
1 large onion, roughly chopped
2 garlic cloves, crushed
400g (14oz) sweet pumpkin or squash, peeled, deseeded and cut into 2.5cm (1in) chunks (prepared weight)

300g (10½oz) tomatoes, roughly chopped
3 tsp smoked paprika
1 tsp chilli flakes (optional)
400g can of white beans, drained and rinsed
1.2 litres (2 pints) chicken stock
300g (10½oz) Spanish paella rice
salt and pepper
2 tbsp chopped flat leaf parsley leaves
lemon wedges, to serve

Put the saffron in a jug, if using, with 50ml (2fl oz) of just-boiled water. Leave for 30 minutes.

Heat the oil in a large deep frying pan, or a broad shallow casserole at least 30cm (12in) in diameter, and brown the sausages. You want to colour them on the outside, not cook them through. Remove and set aside.

Sauté the onion and garlic in the same pan over a medium heat until soft and golden. Add the pumpkin and tomatoes and cook for four minutes. Stir in the paprika and chilli, if using, and cook for a minute, stirring, then tip in the beans and the stock, saffron and its soaking liquid.

Return the sausages to the pan, bring the stock to a simmer and cook over a gentle heat for 10 minutes. Pour the rice round the sausages and season everything well. Cook for 25 minutes, uncovered, but don't stir the rice. All the stock should have been absorbed and the rice should be tender. Sprinkle with parsley and serve with lemon wedges.

baked sausages with apples, raisins & cider

A GREAT COLD WEATHER SUPPER for very little effort. You don't have to soak the raisins in brandy if you feel you don't deserve it (though I'm sure you do); boiling water is fine.

SERVES 6
75g (2½oz) raisins
50ml (2fl oz) brandy (apple brandy or regular brandy, or you can use whiskey)
2 large onions, peeled
3 eating apples, quartered and cored
3 tbsp olive oil
salt and pepper
8 sprigs of thyme
1 tbsp soft light brown sugar
12 pork sausages
200ml (7fl oz) dry cider

Preheat the oven to 190°C/375°F/gas mark 5.

Put the raisins into a saucepan and add the alcohol. Bring to just under the boil, then take the pan off the heat and leave the raisins to plump up for 30 minutes. Halve the onions and cut each half into four wedges. Put the onions and apples into an ovenproof dish that will hold the sausages in a single layer (it makes life easier if it's a dish you can also serve from). Add 2 tbsp of the olive oil, the seasoning and thyme and toss the apples and onions with your hands. Sprinkle sugar on each wedge of apple. Scatter the raisins and their soaking liquid in among the apples.

Heat the remaining 1 tbsp of oil in a frying pan and fry the sausages until golden all over; you are just doing this for colour. Put them on top of the apples and onions and pour in the cider.

Bake for 50 minutes to one hour. The sausages will become dark brown, the apples golden and completely tender and the liquid should be absorbed by the onions. Serve immediately with mash and a green vegetable, such as Savoy cabbage or a watercress salad.

209

smoked sausage with split pea purée & caraway butter

It's amazing what you can do with a packet of split peas. Sometimes I eat the purée here just on its own, with cucumber tossed in sour cream. You could also serve the purée with regular sausages that you've fried, though smoked sausage is easier to get than it used to be. Ocado now sell a French version, that needs to be poached as it is here.

Serves 4

230g (8oz) yellow split peas
1 onion, finely chopped
1 medium carrot, finely chopped
1 leek, white part only, chopped and washed
1 tsp dried marjoram
salt and pepper
1.2 litres (2 pints) mixed stock and water, or just water
1 large smoked sausage, such as Morteau (the usual weight is 350g/12oz)
generous grating of nutmeg
1 tbsp white wine vinegar
50g (1¾oz) unsalted butter
2 tsp caraway seeds

Put the split peas into a saucepan with the onion, carrot, leek, marjoram, seasoning and stock and water, or water. Bring to the boil, reduce the heat to a simmer and cook for about one hour, or until completely soft and a thick purée. When the split peas still have 40 minutes to go, put the sausage into a separate pan of boiling water. Reduce the heat and poach it for 40 minutes.

Return to the purée: add more seasoning (it needs plenty), the nutmeg and vinegar and scrape into a warm bowl. Heat the butter in a frying pan and add the caraway. Cook over a medium heat until you can smell the caraway, but don't let the butter burn, then pour it over the purée.

Slice the sausage and serve with the purée. Warm potatoes tossed with chopped dill pickles, or sliced cucumber mixed with sour cream, are good on the side.

spaghetti with spiced sausage & fennel sauce

EASY, QUICK AND A CROWD PLEASER. My kids love it... and they're pretty picky. Leave out the fennel seeds if you don't have any. You can use pasta shapes instead of spaghetti, if you prefer.

SERVES 4

400g (14oz) spicy pork sausages, preferably Italian

2 tbsp olive oil

1 fennel bulb

1 large onion, finely chopped

½ tsp chilli flakes

pinch of fennel seeds, bashed in a mortar and pestle

2 garlic cloves, crushed

200ml (7fl oz) white or red wine, or dry vermouth

400g can of cherry tomatoes in thick juice

salt and pepper

2 tsp soft light brown sugar

2 tbsp extra virgin olive oil

300g (10½oz) spaghetti

finely grated Parmesan or pecorino cheese, to serve

Remove the sausage casings and form the meat into hazelnut-sized pieces. Heat the regular olive oil in a sauté pan and brown them over a high heat until a good colour all over. Remove from the pan and set aside.

Halve the fennel bulb and take off the tough outer leaves. Trim the tips – keep any little fronds – and cut each piece in half again. Trim the base of each, discard the core, then finely chop. Sauté with the onion over a medium-low heat until soft. Add the chilli, fennel seeds and garlic, plus any fronds, and cook for two minutes. Increase the heat, add the wine and let it bubble until reduced by half. Add the tomatoes, bring to the boil, then reduce the heat to low. Season really well, add the sugar and cook for about 20 minutes, uncovered. Now return the sausage and cook for 15 minutes, stirring from time to time. You may need a little water (it depends how much your sauce has reduced). You should have a good thick sauce that will coat pasta, not a solid purée. Drizzle in the extra virgin olive oil, it's great for extra flavour and enriches the sauce.

Cook the pasta in plenty of boiling salted water until al dente – usually a couple of minutes less than the packet suggests – then drain (not too thoroughly, a little cooking water helps the sauce) and return it to the pan. Stir the sauce into the pasta. Serve with Parmesan or pecorino cheese.

merguez with sweet potatoes, beans & chermoula

THIS IS MOROCCAN INSPIRED; chermoula is a relish that can be used as a sauce or a marinade. Seasoning is important here, as beans are bland without it. It might be a long list of ingredients, but I often make this midweek as it's not taxing, just 15 minutes' work and then into the oven.

SERVES 4

For the sausages
2 tbsp olive oil
8 merguez sausages
1 large onion, roughly chopped
600g (1lb 5oz) sweet potatoes, in chunks
2 garlic cloves, crushed
2 tsp ground cumin
1 tsp ground ginger
¼ tsp chilli flakes
400g can of cherry tomatoes in thick juice
200ml (7fl oz) chicken stock
400g can of cannellini or butter beans, drained
400g can of chickpeas, drained
1 tsp soft light brown sugar (optional)

For the chermoula
5 tbsp extra virgin olive oil
½ tsp ground cumin
½ tsp ground coriander
½ tsp sweet paprika
1 red chilli, deseeded and finely chopped
juice of 1 lemon
1 garlic clove, crushed
15g (½oz) coriander leaves, chopped
2 tbsp chopped flat-leaf parsley

Preheat the oven to 180°C/350°F/gas mark 4. Heat the regular oil in a broad shallow casserole or ovenproof sauté pan (ideally 30cm/12in across) and fry the sausages to get a good colour. Remove and set aside. Add the onion and sauté over a medium heat until golden and soft, about 12 minutes. Add the sweet potatoes and cook for two minutes, then the garlic, cumin and ginger and cook for another two minutes. Stir in the chilli, tomatoes, stock, beans and chickpeas. Season well. Add the sugar, if using (canned tomatoes need it). Bring to the boil, return the sausages, then cook in the oven for one hour. Stir twice during cooking. The sauce will thicken.

Meanwhile, mix everything for the chermoula together. You can spoon this over the finished dish or offer it in a bowl on the side. A bowl of Greek yogurt is good here, too.

CHICKEN

turkish spiced chicken with parsley salad

THE THING ABOUT TURKISH FOOD is that it's incredibly simple, but full of surprises. We don't think of basing a whole salad on parsley – we regard it as a herb, rather than a salad leaf – but this works brilliantly (try it with spiced grilled fish or lamb chops, too).

SERVES 4

For the chicken
75ml (2½fl oz) olive oil
1½ tsp ground cumin
1 tsp ground allspice
1½ tsp Aleppo pepper, or 1 tsp
   cayenne pepper
4 garlic cloves, crushed
salt and pepper
8 skinless boneless chicken thighs
lemon juice and lemon wedges, to serve

For the salad
135g (5oz) tomatoes
very large bunch of parsley, weighing about 115g (4oz)
½ small red onion, very finely chopped
1 small garlic clove, crushed
1 tbsp lemon juice
4 tbsp extra virgin olive oil
1 tbsp pomegranate molasses

Mix the regular olive oil with the spices, garlic and seasoning. Put the chicken in a dish and pour this over it. Cover and put in the fridge to marinate, from 30 minutes up to four hours.

Halve and deseed the tomatoes, then cut the flesh fairly finely (you can skin them too, but I can never be bothered). Chop the parsley leaves finely (use the stalks for something else) and mix with the tomatoes, onion and remaining salad ingredients.

Heat a ridged griddle pan, or a frying pan, until very hot. Lift the chicken out of the marinade, shaking off excess, then cook it: start on a high heat to get a good colour on both sides, then reduce the heat and cook, turning, for about eight minutes in total, or until cooked through. Squeeze lemon juice all over the chicken and serve with lemon wedges and the salad.

chicken piccata

A SIMPLE CLASSIC. Usually this is made with chicken breasts but you can use thighs, too. It's often served with pasta, either plain or try Orzo with lemon & parsley (see page 100).

SERVES 4

2 thick skinless chicken breasts, or 8 small skinless boneless chicken thighs
2 tbsp extra virgin olive oil
25g (scant 1oz) unsalted butter, chilled
salt and pepper
4 tbsp dry vermouth
2 tbsp lemon juice
2½ tbsp capers, rinsed of salt or brine
4 tbsp finely chopped parsley leaves

If you're using chicken breasts, cut them in half horizontally with a sharp knife and put them between two sheets of cling film or greaseproof paper. Bash them with a meat mallet or a rolling pin until slightly flattened. Thighs just need to be opened out.

Heat the oil and one-third of the butter in a large, heavy-based frying pan. Once the butter has foamed, sauté the chicken breasts for two minutes on each side, seasoning as you go, until they are cooked through. You want a good colour on the outside. If you are using thighs, you'll need to cook them for longer. Transfer the chicken to a platter, cover loosely and keep warm.

Add the vermouth and the lemon juice to the frying pan and bring the mixture to the boil. Swirl in the rest of the butter, allowing it to melt, then add the capers and parsley. Check for seasoning: you'll need pepper, but probably not salt. Pour this over the chicken and serve.

orange-oregano roast chicken, olive gremolata

SIMPLE BUT STRIKING looking. Serve with a watercress salad and little potatoes that you've roasted in olive oil or a rice pilaf.

SERVES 6

For the chicken
12 skin-on bone-in chicken thighs
leaves from 1 bunch of oregano, chopped
8 garlic cloves, crushed
juice of 2 oranges and finely grated zest of 1, plus 2 small-medium oranges, preferably thin-skinned, cut into thin slices
5½ tbsp extra virgin olive oil
sea salt flakes and pepper
a little granulated sugar

For the gremolata
200g (7oz) mixed green and black olives, pitted and finely chopped
2 garlic cloves, finely chopped
2 red chillies, deseeded and finely sliced
zest of 1 orange, removed with a zester
leaves from 2 sprigs of oregano, roughly chopped
5 tbsp extra virgin olive oil
1 tbsp orange juice
1 tbsp white balsamic vinegar
squeeze of lemon juice

Trim the chicken thighs of scraggy bits of skin. Pierce the undersides with a sharp knife and put in a dish. Add the oregano, garlic, orange juice and zest, 4 tbsp of the oil and the pepper. Mix with your hands, cover and put in the fridge for a few hours (overnight is even better). For the gremolata, put the olives, garlic, chillies, zest and oregano on a board and finely chop them. Put in a bowl with the rest of the gremolata ingredients and set aside to let the flavours infuse.

Preheat the oven to 190°C/375°F/gas mark 5. Take the chicken out of the marinade, shaking off excess. Heat the remaining 1½ tbsp of oil in a large ovenproof sauté pan or shallow casserole in which the chicken can lie in a single layer. Brown the chicken, in batches, on both sides, finishing skin side up. Scatter with sea salt flakes and roast for 20 minutes.

Lay some of the orange slices under the chicken and the rest on top. Spoon the cooking juices over the oranges, then sprinkle a little sugar over the slices. Roast for another 20 minutes; the chicken and oranges should be cooked. Scatter the gremolata on top. Serve in the roasting dish.

andalusian chicken with honey, saffron & almonds

THIS DISH PRETTY much looks after itself once in the oven. If you
don't like saffron, leave it out, it will still be very good. A picada is used
in Spain to thicken cooking juices and give a final 'lift' to dishes. Don't
worry, it's not overwhelming as the flavours of the garlic and parsley are
softened by the toasted bread.

SERVES 4

For the chicken
generous pinch of saffron strands
1½ tbsp olive oil
8 skin-on bone-in chicken thighs
salt and pepper
2 onions, chopped
2 garlic cloves, crushed
1½ tsp ground ginger
200ml (7fl oz) medium sherry
100ml (3½fl oz) chicken stock or water

juice of 1 small lemon
4½ tbsp runny honey

For the picada
35g (1¼oz) blanched almonds
2 tbsp finely chopped parsley leaves
1 garlic clove, chopped
15g (½oz) fried bread (fried in olive oil),
   broken into chunks
2 tbsp sherry

Put the saffron in a jug and add 50ml (2fl oz) of just-boiled water. Leave to steep for 30 minutes.

Preheat the oven to 200°C/400°F/gas mark 6. Heat the oil in a wide, shallow casserole (30cm/12in
across) in which the chicken can lie in a single layer. Brown the thighs over a medium-high
heat, they don't need to cook through. Season as you go. Remove from the pan. Pour off all but
1½ tbsp of the fat from the pan, put back over a medium heat and cook the onions until golden.
Add the garlic and ginger and cook for two minutes, then add the sherry, saffron with its water
and stock, increase the heat and let it come to the boil. Reduce the heat and add half the lemon
juice and honey. Return the chicken, skin side up, and cook in the oven for 40 minutes. Put
everything for the picada, except the sherry, in a mortar. Bash until coarse. Stir in the sherry.

When the dish has cooked for 30 minutes, mix the remaining lemon and honey and brush it on
to the chicken. Sprinkle the picada around the chicken and cook for the final 10 minutes.

tim's parmesan chicken

MY FRIEND TIM served this for a load of children and adults one weekend and I immediately pounced on the recipe. Now a staple in my house, it's a bung-it-all-in-the-oven dish, the best type for family cooking. If you're in a rush you can skip the marinating bit, just omit the olive oil and add the chopped garlic to the breadcrumb mix instead.

SERVES 4–6

10 good-sized skinless boneless chicken thighs
1½ tbsp olive oil
4 garlic cloves, very finely chopped
salt and pepper
150g (5½oz) white breadcrumbs
15g (½oz) parsley leaves, finely chopped
100g (3½oz) finely grated Parmesan cheese
3 large eggs, lightly beaten

Pierce the chicken all over with a sharp knife. Put it in a shallow dish and rub with the olive oil and garlic. Add pepper, cover and put in the fridge for a few hours if you have the time. If you don't, you can skip this marinating stage (see recipe introduction).

Preheat the oven to 180°C/350°F/gas mark 4; return the chicken to room temperature (if you've marinated it).

Mix the breadcrumbs with the parsley, Parmesan cheese and seasoning. Put this into one broad, flat dish and the eggs into another. Lift the chicken out of the marinade and season all over. Dip each thigh into the eggs and then into the crumbs. Roll each one up – not tightly, just form it roughly into the shape of a thigh – and place in a shallow ovenproof dish. Sprinkle any leftover breadcrumb mixture over the top and pour over the remaining egg.

Cook in the oven for 45 minutes. The top should be golden and the chicken cooked right through. Serve immediately with a green salad and olive oil-roasted potatoes.

moroccan-spiced chicken with dates & aubergines

A USEFUL, NO-HASSLE, chuck-everything-in-together dish, you don't even need to brown the chicken (though make sure you sprinkle the skin with sea salt flakes, to help it crisp up). Find a dish that has about the right dimensions, to ensure that it works well. Don't be afraid of assertive seasoning – rice dishes such as this need it – and don't skip the step where you wash the rice, or it will end up sticky. A bowl of Greek yogurt is good on the side.

SERVES 4–6

225g (8oz) basmati rice

1 large onion, roughly chopped

1 aubergine, cut into cubes

3 garlic cloves, crushed

1 tsp ground ginger

3 tsp ground cumin

4 tsp harissa

finely grated zest and juice of 1 orange

8 skin-on bone-in chicken thighs

12 dates, pitted and sliced

600ml (1 pint) boiling chicken stock

sea salt flakes and pepper

3 tbsp olive oil

15g (½oz) chopped pistachio nuts

Preheat the oven to 200°C/400°F/gas mark 6.

Put the rice into a sieve and wash it in running water until the water runs clear. Tip it into an ovenproof dish which will hold the chicken in a single layer (I use a heavy-based shallow casserole, 30cm/12in in diameter). Add everything else, except the oil and pistachio nuts, and toss around to mix, leaving the chicken pieces skin side up and sprinkling them with salt.

Drizzle on the oil. Cook in the oven, uncovered, for 40 minutes. The top should be golden and the chicken cooked through. Sprinkle on the pistachio nuts and serve with a green salad.

korean chicken, gochujang mayo & sweet-sour cucumber

GOD, THIS IS GOOD. I made it for Bonfire Night one year as it's great 'hold in the hand' food… and it's never been off the menu since. The chicken must be warm – not hot – or the mayo turns oily. Gochujang is Korean chilli paste; it has a special flavour, sweet and hot with a hint of miso.

SERVES 6

For the chicken and marinade
3 fat garlic cloves, crushed
200ml (7fl oz) soy sauce
4 tbsp light brown sugar
2 tsp rice vinegar
50ml (2fl oz) sesame oil
8–12 skinless boneless chicken thighs

For the mayonnaise
135g (4¾oz) mayonnaise
2 tsp gochujang
½ garlic clove, finely grated to a purée
good squeeze of lime juice, to taste

For the sweet-sour cucumber
1 ridge cucumber
1 shallot, very finely sliced
4 tbsp rice vinegar, or to taste
3 tsp caster sugar, or to taste
1 red chilli, deseeded and finely sliced

To serve
6 bread rolls or wraps, warmed
sprigs of coriander

Mix all the ingredients for the chicken. Turn the chicken in this marinade, cover and chill for four hours or so, turning every so often. For the mayonnaise, just mix the mayo, gochujang and garlic. Add lime juice to taste. Peel the cucumber, halve it lengthways, scoop out and discard the seeds. Slice finely, then mix it with the rest of its ingredients, adding 1½ tbsp of water. Leave for 30 minutes. Taste for sweet-sour balance, adding more vinegar or sugar if you like.

Lift the chicken out of the marinade, shaking off excess. Heat a couple of frying pans. Cook on a high heat for a couple of minutes, turning frequently, then reduce the heat and cook until done right through (check by cutting into one of the thicker pieces) and lovely and dark gold. Put the chicken on a plate – add the juices as well, so the chicken stays moist – and leave to cool a little.

Fill the warm rolls or wraps with chicken, coriander and cucumber. Slather with mayo. Serve.

chicken with haricots & creamy basil dressing

BEST LUKEWARM rather than hot, so it's good for summer. You can poach the chicken rather than sautéing (though remove the skin before serving if you poach it). Make the dressing just before you start the dish, as it discolours if it sits for long. Don't get whacking great chicken breasts, medium-sized are better here.

SERVES 4

For the dressing
50g (1¾oz) basil leaves
½ small garlic clove, crushed
¾ tbsp white balsamic vinegar
salt and pepper
6 tbsp extra virgin olive oil (fruity, not bitter)
6 tbsp double cream
1½ tbsp lemon juice, or to taste

For the chicken
3 tbsp olive oil
4 chicken breasts, skin on or off, as you like
150g (5½oz) green beans, topped but not tailed
2 shallots, finely sliced
400g can of haricot beans, drained and rinsed
150g (5½oz) cherry tomatoes, halved
½ tbsp lemon juice
2 tbsp extra virgin olive oil

Make the dressing: put the basil into a food processor with the garlic, vinegar, seasoning and extra virgin olive oil. Whizz until blended. Scrape into a bowl and stir in the cream and lemon juice. The mixture will thicken, so you may want to add a little water to let it down again. (Not too much, though. I like this spoonable rather than pourable.) Check the seasoning.

Now on to the chicken. Heat the regular olive oil in a large frying pan, season the chicken and fry it, (skin side down if it's skin on), for four or five minutes, over a medium-high heat to get a good colour, then reduce the heat. Turn and cook for another four or five minutes. Cut into the chicken on the underside to check for doneness; the juices should be clear with no trace of pink. Set aside.

Boil or steam the green beans until tender but still al dente. Put these, the shallots, haricot beans and tomatoes in a bowl and season well. Stir in the lemon juice and extra virgin olive oil. Divide between four plates and put a chicken breast on each. Spoon over the basil dressing.

parmesan roast chicken with cauliflower & thyme

THIS CAME ABOUT because I had a craving for roast chicken with cauliflower cheese one night, but was too lazy to make it. The whole family fell for it and it has since become a staple. You could use a mixture of cheeses – half Gruyère to replace some of the Parmesan, for example – if you want something more melting and gooey on top.

SERVES 4

8 skin-on bone-in chicken thighs

350g (12oz) baby waxy potatoes, halved

1 cauliflower, broken into good-sized florets

2 onions, cut into wedges

8 sprigs of thyme

4 tbsp extra virgin olive oil

sea salt flakes and pepper

30g (1oz) Parmesan cheese, finely grated

Preheat the oven to 200°C/400°F/gas mark 6.

Put the chicken, potatoes, cauliflower and onions into a roasting tin in which everything can lie in a single layer, or the chicken and vegetables will sweat instead of roasting. Tear in the thyme, pour in the oil and season. Toss everything around with your hands, finishing with the chicken skin side up. Sprinkle sea salt flakes on the chicken, to help the skin to crisp up.

Roast, tossing occasionally – you have to ensure that the cauliflower gets golden all over, not just on one side – for 35 minutes. Sprinkle with the Parmesan cheese, toss to combine and roast for another 10 minutes. The chicken and potatoes should be cooked through, the onions slightly scorched at the tips, and the surface of everything golden.

burmese chicken with tart-sweet chilli sauce

THIS IS FROM one of my favourite books, *Burma: Rivers of Flavor*, by Naomi Duguid. I've fiddled a little with the sauce, but that's it. This is one of the most addictive and easy dishes in the book. If you're not familiar with Naomi's work, seek it out. I have every book she's written.

SERVES 6

For the chicken
1.3kg (3lb) skinless boneless chicken thighs
1 tsp ground turmeric
½ tsp salt
½ tsp cayenne pepper
2cm (¾in) piece of root ginger, peeled
    and grated
4 garlic cloves, grated
2 tbsp fish sauce
2 tbsp groundnut oil

For the dipping sauce
10g (¼oz) dried red chillies (remove the
    seeds from half of them)
3 garlic cloves, finely chopped
1 tbsp fish sauce
3 tbsp caster sugar
2 tbsp rice vinegar
really good squeeze of lime juice, plus
    lime wedges to serve

Put the chicken thighs in a dish and mix in all the other ingredients except the oil. Turn the meat over until completely coated. Cover and put in the fridge to marinate for 30 minutes, then return to room temperature.

Meanwhile, to make the dipping sauce, put the chillies in a saucepan with 200ml (7fl oz) of water. Bring to the boil, then reduce the heat and simmer for three to five minutes. Mix this (including the water) with all the other ingredients and either pulse-blend in a small food processor or pound in a mortar and pestle (you need to break down the chillies and garlic).

Heat the oil in a frying pan and cook the chicken in batches. You need to start off over a high heat to get a good colour, then reduce the heat to medium-low to cook it through. Keep turning the chicken as it cooks. Serve with lime wedges and the dipping sauce and boiled rice.

chicken chettinad

INDIAN FOOD has a hard time when it comes to quick cooking, as nearly every dish has quite a few ingredients. I now keep a tin on my kitchen counter with all my most used spices in it; that makes life a lot easier. This dish actually tastes better the day after you cook it. Because it contains yogurt, don't boil it, though, instead bring it to just under the boil when you are reheating it, otherwise the sauce will split.

SERVES 4

For the chicken
550g (1lb 4oz) skinless boneless chicken thighs, cut into big chunks
200g (7oz) plain yogurt
1½ tsp ground turmeric
½ tsp salt
2 tbsp vegetable oil
2 onions, finely chopped
1 tsp fennel seeds
1 cinnamon stick

8 garlic cloves, grated
5cm (2in) root ginger, peeled and grated
1 tsp soft dark brown sugar
1 tbsp roughly chopped coriander leaves

For the spice blend
¾ tbsp fennel seeds
¾ tbsp coriander seeds
½ tbsp black peppercorns
1 tsp chilli flakes

Put the chicken in a bowl with the yogurt, turmeric and salt and stir together. Cover and leave to marinate for 30 minutes. Put all the spices for the spice blend in a dry frying pan over a medium heat and stir until they smell aromatic. Grind them in a small blender, or by bashing in a mortar and pestle.

Heat the oil in a small casserole or sauté pan and cook the onions until they are soft and golden. Add the fennel seeds and cinnamon stick and cook for a couple of minutes, then add the chicken, garlic, ginger and spice blend. Turn everything over with a wooden spoon and cook for four minutes, then add the sugar and 100ml (3½fl oz) of water and bring to a gentle simmer.

Cook very gently for 15 minutes – the juices will thicken a bit as the dish cooks – then scatter with the coriander and serve with rice and chutney.

chicken with indian spices, mango & coconut

I FIND THE COMBINATION of spices, mango and coconut absolutely irresistible. And yes I am suggesting you use curry paste, otherwise it means an endless list of spices. Why make life hard? This dish works perfectly well with a paste.

SERVES 4

10g (¼oz) unsalted butter

½ tbsp groundnut oil

6 skinless boneless chicken thighs, cut in half

salt and pepper

2 medium onions, roughly chopped

3 garlic cloves, crushed

6 medium tomatoes, chopped

1½ tbsp curry paste (I use Patak's vindaloo)

1 tsp ground ginger

250ml (9fl oz) chicken stock

160ml can of coconut cream

1 tsp soft light brown sugar

1 just-ripe mango, peeled, pitted and sliced

3 tbsp double cream

juice of ½ lemon or 2 limes

2 tbsp roughly chopped coriander leaves

Heat the butter and oil in a sauté pan, add the chicken and cook until golden on both sides, seasoning it as it cooks. (You only want to colour it, not cook it through.) Remove to a plate.

Add the onions and garlic to the pan and cook over a medium heat until soft, about 10 minutes. Tip in the tomatoes and cook for another three minutes. Stir in the curry paste and ginger. Cook for two minutes, until the spices have released their aromas, then add the stock, bring to the boil and keep boiling until the liquid has been reduced by about half.

Reduce the heat, add the coconut cream and sugar and return the chicken to the pan. Cook over a medium-low heat – don't boil it – for 15 minutes. Add the mango in the last four minutes of cooking time.

Stir in the cream and add the citrus juice. Taste for seasoning. Simmer for about a minute to heat through, then add the coriander and serve with rice.

VEGETABLES

roast squash with ricotta, smoked cheese & sage

A CROWN PRINCE squash is the one to go for here, it has a lovely colour and a good sweet flavour. Do try to buy fresh ricotta, rather than the UHT stuff; you'll find it in delis or specialist Italian shops. Godminster make a gorgeous oak-smoked Cheddar.

SERVES 6

For the salad
1.5kg (3lb 5oz) squash or pumpkin
6 tbsp olive oil
freshly grated nutmeg
300g (10½oz) fresh ricotta
150g (5½oz) salad leaves, such as baby spinach, ruby chard or watercress, coarse stalks removed
100g (3½oz) smoked cheese, shaved
18–24 sage leaves

For the dressing
¾ tbsp white balsamic vinegar
smidgen of Dijon mustard
4 tbsp extra virgin olive oil
salt and pepper

Preheat the oven to 190°C/375°F/gas mark 5. Halve the squash, deseed and slice the flesh into wedges about 2cm (¾in) thick at their widest. Peel each wedge. Put the slices into a roasting tin with 4½ tbsp of the olive oil, the nutmeg and salt and pepper and toss to coat in the seasoning and oil. Roast for about 25 minutes, or until tender and slightly caramelized in places.

Make the dressing by whisking everything together, then season well. Break the ricotta into little chunks with a fork. Toss the leaves with two-thirds of the dressing and divide between six plates or put on one big platter. Add the roast squash, ricotta and shaved smoked cheese.

Heat the rest of the olive oil in a frying pan and quickly sauté the sage leaves until they are crisp. Scatter these over the top, then drizzle with the rest of the dressing and serve.

broccoli with harissa & coriander gremolata

When purple-sprouting broccoli isn't in season, use regular calabrese or Tenderstem broccoli instead. This is also lovely made with roast cauliflower (see page 244 for how to roast cauliflower).

Serves 6 as a side dish

For the broccoli
100g (3½oz) unsalted butter, at room temperature
3½ tsp harissa
pinch of salt
squeeze of lime juice
30 purple-sprouting broccoli spears

For the gremolata
1 small garlic clove, roughly chopped
3 tbsp chopped coriander leaves
zest of 2 limes, removed with a zester

Mash the butter with the harissa, salt and lime juice. Cook the broccoli – either boiling or steaming it – until just tender (test with the tip of a small sharp knife). The time it takes depends on the thickness of the spears.

Finely chop the ingredients for the gremolata together so that they're combined. Remove the broccoli spears from the pan and immediately put them into a clean tea towel, to soak up some of the excess moisture. Put on to a warm platter with knobs of the butter.

Allow the butter to melt a little, then scatter on the gremolata.

ginger-miso pumpkin & mushrooms, black sesame

A LOVELY MIXTURE of sweetness, earthiness and lip-smacking umami. I sometimes make a little extra of the miso mixture and use it to dress purple-sprouting broccoli (which I add to this dish at the end). Brown rice is lovely on the side. This is so satisfying, you won't even think about meat.

SERVES 6

1.3kg (3lb) pumpkin, such as Crown Prince, deseeded, cut into wedges and peeled

2cm (¾in) root ginger, peeled and grated

2 garlic cloves, grated

¼ tsp chilli flakes

6 tbsp groundnut oil

salt and pepper

3 tbsp white miso

1½ tbsp honey

2 tbsp rice vinegar

3 tsp soy sauce

400g (14oz) large flat mushrooms (about 6)

55g (2oz) baby spinach leaves

generous squeeze of lime juice

¼ tbsp black sesame seeds

Preheat the oven to 200°C/400°F/gas mark 6. Put the pumpkin into a roasting tin, it needs to lie in a (more or less) single layer. Mix the ginger, garlic, chilli, 4½ tbsp of the oil and seasoning and add it to the pumpkin, turning to make sure it is well coated. Roast for 30 minutes. Mix the miso, honey, rice vinegar and soy sauce together with 1½ tbsp of warm water.

Arrange the mushrooms in a separate roasting tin and add the remaining 1½ tbsp of the oil, turning the mushrooms over in it. Put one-third of the miso mixture on the mushrooms and put them into the oven. Add the rest of the miso to the pumpkin, turning all the vegetables over in it. Roast for another 30 minutes along with the mushrooms.

At the end of cooking time, add the spinach to the pumpkin and turn it over in the cooking juices; it should wilt a little in the heat. Transfer all the vegetables to a warm, broad, shallow serving bowl. Squeeze some lime juice over the whole dish and scatter the sesame seeds on top.

roast sweet & bitter vegetables, salsa bianca

I LOVE THE TASTES of bitter and sweet together, and it's even better when there's something salty added to the mix. This sauce is Italian, but I do sometimes make it with Scandinavian sweet-cured anchovies. The result is different, but also very good.

SERVES 8 as a side dish, 4 as a main course

For the vegetables
8 carrots, halved lengthways (quartered if very fat)
650g (1lb 7oz) cauliflower, broken into florets
2 beetroots (not too big), trimmed and cut into wedges
about 8 sprigs of thyme
3 onions, cut into thick wedges
6 tbsp olive oil
salt and pepper
1 head of radicchio, cut into 6 wedges
2 heads of red or white chicory, quartered

For the salsa bianca
75g (2¾oz) pine nuts
50g can of anchovies in olive oil, drained
1 fat garlic clove, crushed
100ml (3½fl oz) extra virgin olive oil
lemon juice, to taste

Preheat the oven to 190°C/375°F/gas mark 5. Put the carrots, cauliflower, beetroots, thyme and onion wedges into a roasting tin in which they can lie in a single layer: you want them to roast, not sweat. Drizzle with the regular olive oil, season and turn the vegetables over to make sure they all get well coated. Roast for about 25 minutes, turning them over every so often, then brush the radicchio and chicory with a little more regular olive oil and add to the tin. Roast for another 15 minutes, or until all the vegetables are tender and slightly burnished in patches.

To make the salsa, dry-fry the pine nuts in a frying pan until golden and smelling toasted. Tip into a mortar and pound with the anchovies and garlic, then start adding the extra virgin olive oil, a little at a time. Season and add the lemon juice to taste. You should have a rough paste. It's strong, but good with this. Serve the vegetables with the salsa on the side.

roast cauliflower with spanish flavours

I ATE A DISH very like this at Opera Tavern in Covent Garden in London and couldn't get it out of my head. I tried to recreate it quite a few times, but something always seemed missing, so I contacted the chef, Ben Tish, and he gave me his recipe. The following is a blend of both our approaches. If you like it, the credit goes to Ben.

SERVES 4 as a side dish or 'small plate'

75g (2¾oz) raisins

200ml (7fl oz) amontillado sherry

1 large head of cauliflower, broken into good-sized florets

2 onions, cut into 2.5cm (1in) wedges

8 sprigs of thyme

½ tsp ground cinnamon

1 tsp cumin seeds

5 tbsp extra virgin olive oil, or to taste

salt and pepper

2 garlic cloves, finely sliced

¼ tsp chilli flakes

½ tbsp sherry vinegar

good squeeze of lemon juice, or to taste

25g (scant 1oz) toasted pine nuts (see page 242)

Put the raisins in a saucepan with the sherry and bring to the boil. As soon as it reaches the boil, take the pan off the heat and leave the raisins to plump up for about 30 minutes.

Preheat the oven to 200°C/400°F/gas mark 6. Put the cauliflower and onions into a roasting tin in which everything can lie in a single layer. Tear in the thyme roughly and add the cinnamon, cumin, 3 tbsp of the olive oil and seasoning. Toss all this round with your hands and put it in the oven for 35 minutes. Toss occasionally: you have to ensure the cauliflower becomes golden all over, not just on one side.

Halfway through cooking, add the garlic, chilli and raisins with their soaking liquid and mix. When the cauliflower is tender and golden, remove it from the oven. Set the roasting tin over a medium heat and add the sherry vinegar, the rest of the olive oil and the lemon juice. Gently toss around and warm through. Taste: you might find you need a little more lemon juice or oil, or to adjust the seasoning. Transfer to a warm platter, scatter with the pine nuts and serve.

peperoni gratinati al forno

JUST WHEN YOU THOUGHT you were aware of everything that could be done with roast peppers, along comes this from the south of Italy. I've described it as a side dish (it is great with lamb) but, in fact, a lunch of these peppers – served tepid – with burrata is more feast than side dish.

SERVES 6 as a side dish

8 red peppers, halved and deseeded, stems removed

extra virgin olive oil

8 cured anchovies, drained and chopped

15g (½oz) black olives, pitted and chopped

2 tbsp capers, rinsed

leaves from 2 sprigs of oregano, torn

2 small garlic cloves, grated

¼ tsp chilli flakes (optional)

35g (1¼oz) stale breadcrumbs

Preheat the oven to 180°C/350°F/gas mark 4. Put the peppers into a roasting tin, brush with olive oil and cook in the hot oven for 30 minutes. Remove from the oven.

Increase the oven temperature to 190°C/375°F/gas mark 5.

Cut the peppers into strips and toss with the rest of the ingredients in a bowl, keeping some breadcrumbs back for the top. Put into a gratin dish or other shallow ovenproof dish. Sprinkle with the rest of the crumbs, drizzle with more olive oil and put back into the oven for another 15 minutes, or until the crumbs are golden. Serve.

sweet potatoes with yogurt & coriander-chilli sauce

HOT, SWEET, COOL, all the contrasts I love are in this dish. You can use the yogurt and sauce for baked sweet potatoes, just split them and fill with a spoonful of each.

SERVES 6 as a side dish

For the sweet potatoes
1kg (2lb 4oz) sweet potatoes, scrubbed really
   well and cut into thick wedges
4 tbsp olive oil
½ tbsp honey
juice of 1 lime
salt and pepper
250g (9oz) Greek yogurt
extra virgin olive oil

For the sauce
2 garlic cloves, chopped
2 green chillies, deseeded and chopped
20g (¾oz) blanched almonds
leaves from 1 medium bunch of coriander,
   about 15g (½oz)
5 tbsp extra virgin olive oil
juice of 1 lime
1 tbsp white balsamic vinegar

Preheat the oven to 180°C/350°F/gas mark 4.

Put the sweet potatoes into a roasting tin. Mix together the regular olive oil, honey, lime juice and seasoning and toss this with the potato wedges. Cook for 30–35 minutes, until tender.

Put everything for the sauce into a food processor and pulse-blend, to form a rough purée. Put the potatoes into a warm serving dish. Spoon the herb sauce and some of the yogurt over the wedges, drizzle with extra virgin olive oil and serve with the rest of the yogurt.

creamy gratin of rainbow chard & red chicory

I LOVE A CREAMY vegetable gratin – who doesn't? – but they can be a little cloying. In this dish, chicory's slight bitterness cuts through the richness. You can leave out the anchovies if you hate them, but they don't taste fishy once it's all cooked, they just end up giving the dish a bit of an umami hit.

SERVES 4 as a side dish

500g (1lb 2oz) rainbow chard or regular chard

15g (½oz) unsalted butter

salt and pepper

1 small onion, finely chopped

olive oil

1 small head of red chicory, leaves separated and chopped

4 anchovies, drained and chopped

1 garlic clove, crushed

250ml (9fl oz) double cream

80g (2¾oz) finely grated Parmesan cheese

15g (½oz) breadcrumbs

Preheat the oven to 200°C/400°F/gas mark 6.

Pull the leafy bits off the chard, trim the stalks and cut them into 4cm (1½in) lengths. Put the stalks in a big pan of boiling water and cook for three minutes, adding the leaves after two minutes. Drain. Dry the leafy bits in a tea towel (but don't squeeze them as you might spinach).

Melt the butter in a frying pan, add a little salt and sauté the onion for about six minutes, until soft but not coloured. Add a splash of olive oil and the chicory, anchovies and garlic and cook until the chicory has softened, about three minutes. Now put the chard leaves and stems into the pan and turn them around to get well-flavoured in the fat. If the chard is still a bit watery, increase the heat to high to drive off the moisture. Reduce the heat to medium again and pour in the cream, then add 60g (2¼oz) of the Parmesan cheese and plenty of pepper (you probably won't need salt because of the anchovies, but taste to check).

Transfer the mixture to a gratin dish, sprinkle with the remaining Parmesan cheese and the breadcrumbs and bake for 20–30 minutes. The top should be golden.

olive oil-braised leeks & peas with feta & dill

USE CRUMBLED RICOTTA and mint here instead of feta and dill, if you prefer. Just be sure to cook the leeks gently. I've suggested having this as a side dish, but actually it makes a lovely main course with another vegetable dish and couscous or bulgar wheat.

SERVES 4 as a side dish, or as a main course with a spread of other vegetable dishes

4 large leeks
75ml (2½fl oz) extra virgin olive oil, plus more to serve
75ml (2½fl oz) light chicken or vegetable stock
1 garlic clove, crushed
salt and pepper
165g (5¾oz) peas, fresh or frozen (podded weight, if fresh)
finely grated zest of ½ unwaxed lemon
1 tbsp roughly chopped dill fronds
100g (3½oz) feta cheese, crumbled

Remove the coarser outer leaves from the leeks and trim the tops. Cut into 4cm (1½in) lengths, discarding the bases. Wash really well, so you get rid of any trapped soil.

Heat the oil in a heavy-based saucepan or sauté pan and gently cook the leeks over a medium heat for about seven minutes. Don't let them colour. Add the stock and garlic, bring to the boil, then immediately reduce the heat to low, season and cover with a lid. Cook for 10–12 minutes, until the leeks are just tender (check with the point of a knife).

Add the peas and cook until they are tender (frozen peas need very little cooking, they more or less just heat through). Sprinkle on the lemon zest and check for seasoning. Transfer to a bowl – a shallow dish looks best – and scatter with the dill and feta. Drizzle with more oil and serve.

tomatoes, potatoes & vermouth with basil crème fraîche

BAKING WAXY POTATOES can be problematic. They seem to become tender at different rates depending on the variety, so you may have to cook this a little longer than suggested. You want to end up with the right amount of liquid, too, as the vegetables should be just coated in thickish juices, not swimming in them. It's a simple dish, but requires a bit of judgement.

SERVES 6 as a side dish

2 red onions, halved

600g (1lb 5oz) baby waxy potatoes, halved lengthways

800g (1lb 12oz) plum tomatoes, halved

6 tbsp extra virgin olive oil

3 tbsp white balsamic vinegar

finely grated zest of 1 unwaxed lemon, plus juice of ½

4 garlic cloves, crushed

salt and pepper

100ml (3½fl oz) dry vermouth

300ml (½ pint) crème fraîche

leaves from a small bunch of basil, torn

Preheat the oven to 210°C/440°F/gas mark 6½. Cut the onions into crescent-shaped wedges (about 2cm/¾in at their thickest part) and put them into an ovenproof and flameproof dish big enough to hold all the vegetables in a single layer (a really big roasting tin is good). Add the potatoes, tomatoes, oil, vinegar, lemon zest, garlic and seasoning and toss everything around with your hands. Finish with the tomatoes cut sides up.

Roast for 45–60 minutes, pouring in the vermouth 20 minutes before the end of cooking time. (Waxy potatoes vary in the length of time they take to cook, and they need to be tender.) There will probably be liquid – vermouth and cooking juices – round the vegetables. Put the dish over a high heat on the hob and simmer until some of this has boiled off. It doesn't matter if the tomatoes get softer and lose their shape as you do this.

Check the seasoning and transfer to a heated serving dish. Mix the crème fraîche with the lemon juice and basil. Serve the vegetables with the cream.

asparagus, goat's cheese & warm butter

DON'T USE STRONG goat's cheese for this, it would overwhelm the delicate asparagus. A milder cheese, creamy or chalky in texture, is what you want.

SERVES 4 as a main course, 6 as a starter
1kg (2lb 4oz) asparagus spears
75g (2¾oz) unsalted butter
juice of 1 lemon
350g (12oz) rindless goat's cheese, broken into chunks
salt and pepper

Break or cut the woody ends from the asparagus spears. Bring about 7.5cm (3in) of water to the boil in a saucepan and put the bases of the asparagus spears in this, leaning the upper parts against the side of the pan (or use an asparagus cooker if you have one, or steam them). Cook until just tender but still a little firm; it should take about four minutes, but it depends on the thickness of the spears.

Meanwhile, melt the butter and add the lemon juice to it. Lift the asparagus out and drain before dividing between individual plates (or serve on a platter). Scatter the cheese over the top, sprinkle with salt and pepper and pour on some of the lemon butter. Put the rest of the butter in a jug and serve with good bread.

artichokes, carrots & preserved lemons with ginger & honey

AN INTERESTING DISH. Instead of bunging all the ingredients – without liquid – into the oven, I tried something more like a vegetable braise, but didn't cook it on the stove top. It has Moroccan flavours – preserved lemons, honey – but French touches, too (bay and vermouth). I can eat this on its own as a main course, but it's also a lovely side dish for lamb. You can add peas or broad beans, but that rather ruins the muted colours.

SERVES 6 as a main course

300g (10½oz) young carrots, ideally slim
500g (1lb 2oz) baby waxy potatoes, halved
12 shallots, peeled and halved
1 head of garlic, cloves separated and peeled
½ tbsp peeled and finely grated root ginger
¾ tsp Aleppo pepper or cayenne pepper
1 tsp coriander seeds, roughly crushed
about 6 sprigs of thyme, plus leaves from 2 more

3 preserved lemons, flesh discarded, rind shredded
4 bay leaves
100ml (3½fl oz) extra virgin olive oil
100ml (3½fl oz) vermouth
400ml (14fl oz) vegetable stock
400g can of artichoke hearts, drained
2 tbsp honey

Preheat the oven to 180°C/350°F/gas mark 4. Peel the carrots and trim the tops. If they're slim leave them whole, otherwise halve them lengthways. Put everything – except the artichokes, extra thyme leaves and honey – into a big roasting tin. The vegetables should lie in a single layer. Set over a medium heat and bring the liquid just to the boil. Immediately put it into the oven and cook for 45 minutes. Gently turn the vegetables over once or twice during this time.

Drain and dry the artichoke hearts in kitchen paper, then halve them. Add to the vegetables and cook for a further 15 minutes. Drizzle the honey over, scatter on the remaining thyme and cook for a final 15 minutes. You should have soft vegetables with olive oil-rich, well-reduced juices.

salty baked potatoes with yogurt

I KNOW THIS MIGHT SEEM RIDICULOUS: a recipe for baked potatoes. But there is a right way to do them, so that you end up with a crisp skin and a fluffy interior. They might be simple, but they're worth doing well.

SERVES 6

6 medium floury potatoes, weighing about 300g (10½oz) each (King Edward, Desirée, Maris Piper, Wilja, Golden Wonder and Cara are all good varieties for baking)
sea salt flakes and pepper
unsalted butter
Greek yogurt

Preheat the oven to 200°C/400°F/gas mark 6.

Scrub the potatoes and prick with a fork. While they are still damp, sprinkle lightly all over with the sea salt flakes. This gives a crisp skin (cooking them wrapped in foil would give a soft skin).

Put the potatoes on a baking sheet – they shouldn't touch each other – then wet your hands and splash the baking sheet with water. Bake in the oven for 1–1½ hours (the exact cooking time depends on size and how many potatoes you are cooking at once; a bigger quantity of potatoes sometimes takes longer). To test whether the potato is done, press it: it should feel soft under the skin and 'give' a little. You can put a fine skewer right through to the centre of the potato if you want to be sure.

Make a cross in the top with a sharp knife and firmly press the potato (hold it in a tea towel while you do this) so it opens at all four points. Season with salt and pepper and put a knob of butter in the middle, then a dollop of yogurt.

one potato, two potato...

The first baked potatoes I ever tasted – odd for an Irish girl – were in Canada. I thought the mix of hot potato flesh, melting butter, cool sour cream and chopped spring onion was irresistible. At university – where a weekly essay crisis required all-night working – I'd trudge to the spud van on the High Street at about 2am. When there was frost or snow underfoot you couldn't wait to get your hands round the warm Styrofoam box. Shovelling in potato, baked beans and grated cheese was so comforting. It's often hard, when you're hungry, to think of interesting fillings for baked spuds, though. So here's a few of my favourites. I still have baked beans and Cheddar cheese – it tastes of the past, apart from anything else – but I can often do a bit better than that.

CASHEL BLUE, WALNUTS & WATERCRESS
Split open your potato. Fill with a handful of watercress (it will wilt and that's fine), a dollop of sour cream, crumbled Cashel blue cheese or Roquefort and a sprinkle of toasted walnuts.

SOUR CREAM, SMOKED TROUT & DILL
A classic and as good as ever, but best in smaller potatoes (it seems very rich in a big spud). Put a knob of butter in your split potato, then sour cream, flaked smoked trout and chopped dill. To be indulgent, a spoon of keta (salmon roe) is gorgeous on top.

BACON LARDONS, ONIONS & GRUYERE
Fry bacon lardons – chunky ones – in the fat that runs out of them as they cook. Set aside and sauté finely sliced onions in the fat until soft and golden (or take them to dark gold by increasing the heat). Fill your split potato with the onions, bacon and, finally, grated Gruyère cheese. To get the Gruyère to melt into those gorgeous long strings, put the potato under a hot grill. This is pretty good with a fried or poached egg on top as well (what a feast).

DAL, YOGURT & SPICY BUTTER
My student standby dish. But I make it better now. Make some dal (see page 77); you don't have to use pumpkin, just increase the amount of lentils. Fill a potato with this, natural yogurt (not Greek) and chopped coriander. Melt butter in a frying pan and add cumin seeds and chilli flakes, plus chopped ginger and garlic if you can be bothered. Pour over the yogurt.

YOGURT, AVOCADO SALSA & FETA
Fill a baked sweet potato with a big spoonful of Greek yogurt and another of chopped avocado mixed with chopped tomatoes, lime juice, chilli, ground cumin and olive oil. Top with chopped coriander leaves and roughly crumbled feta cheese.

GOAT'S CHEESE & BLACK OLIVE RELISH
Chop pitted black olives and mix them with chopped walnuts, parsley, garlic, chilli, olive oil and white balsamic vinegar. Squeeze on some lemon juice. Put crumbled goat's cheese and rocket leaves into a split baked sweet potato and spoon the relish on top. Grind on pepper.

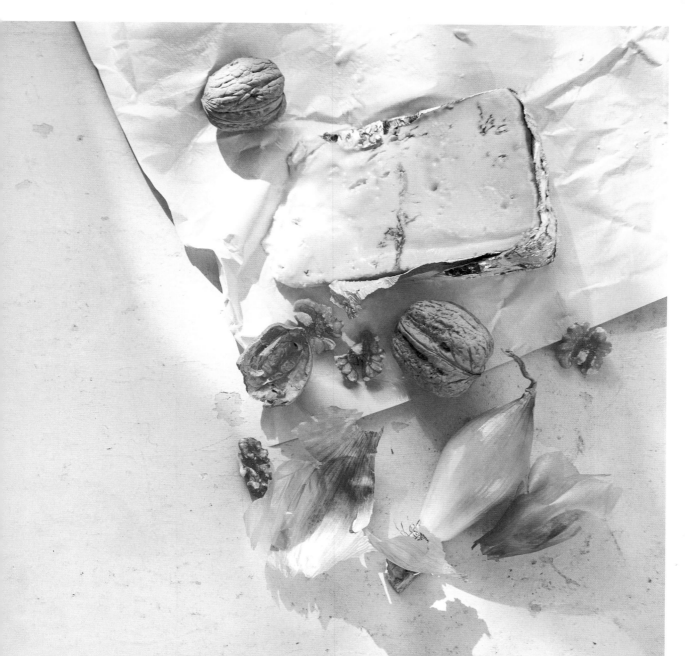

HAM, CAMEMBERT & CREAM

Bake your potato, then take the flesh out of it
and mash it. Cook some finely chopped onion
in butter, then add cooked ham (the chunks
you get at the deli counter are good), seasoning
and cream. Mix with chopped camembert (or
grated Cheddar or Gruyère) cheese and return
to the potato cases. Grill or bake until golden.

SMOKED HADDOCK, CHEDDAR & SPINACH

Poach smoked haddock in milk until almost
cooked. Wilt spinach in butter and cook until
the water mostly evaporates. Chop. Mash the
spinach with the flesh from the baked potatoes,
the haddock, butter, some cream, seasoning
and grated Cheddar cheese. Pile back into the
cases and brown under the grill.

baked sweet potato, chorizo, mushrooms & egg

SWEET *and* earthy, always a winning combination. You can leave the egg off, or use bacon lardons instead of chorizo, if you prefer. A great, gooey, savoury-sweet plateful.

SERVES 2

2 sweet potatoes
3 tbsp extra virgin olive oil
150g (5½oz) chestnut mushrooms, cleaned, chopped into pieces
salt and pepper
100g (3½oz) chorizo, sliced a little thicker than a £1 coin
2 large eggs
small handful of coriander leaves (optional)
sprinkling of smoked paprika (optional)

Preheat the oven to 200°C/400°F/gas mark 6.

You bake sweet potatoes in the same way as regular potatoes, but for only about 30 minutes (though I find cooking time varies according to the texture of the variety you're using). Be careful to bake them in a foil-lined tin, as they leach a sticky liquid that is hell to shift.

When the potatoes are nearly cooked, heat 1 tbsp of the olive oil in a frying pan and sauté the mushrooms briskly over a fairly high heat. Season. Mushrooms give out a lot of moisture when they cook, so make sure these juices have evaporated. Scrape into a bowl and keep warm. Add ½ tbsp more oil to the pan and brown the chorizo on both sides. Add to the mushrooms.

Heat the rest of the oil and fry the eggs, scooping hot oil up over the yolks to help them cook.

Split each potato lengthways to open them up. Spoon the mushrooms and chorizo inside the potatoes and scatter with the coriander. Top with the fried eggs – sprinkling on a little smoked paprika, if you want – and serve with baby leaves, such as spinach.

butternut strata

A STRATA IS an Italian savoury bread pudding, a generous, melting dishful which is great for lunch or supper with friends. If you want a vegetarian version, just leave out the bacon and use more squash. You can add cooked leeks or spinach, but make sure they're well drained.

SERVES 8

1kg (2lb 4oz) butternut squash
3½ tbsp olive oil, plus more for the sage
salt and pepper
250g (9oz) ricotta, preferably fresh, not UHT
40g (1½oz) sourdough bread (weighed without crusts)
450ml (16fl oz) whole milk
6 large eggs, lightly beaten

generous grating of nutmeg
about 15 sage leaves
60g (2¼oz) Parmesan or pecorino, finely grated
1 onion, finely chopped
2 garlic cloves, finely chopped
200g (7oz) bacon lardons
unsalted butter, for the dish
125g (4½oz) buffalo mozzarella, drained, torn

Preheat the oven to 200°C/400°F/gas mark 6. Deseed the squash and cut into 2.5cm (1in) wedges. Peel and put into a roasting tin. Toss with 2 tbsp of the olive oil and season. Roast until tender and slightly caramelized (about 35 minutes). Allow to cool. Drain the ricotta in a sieve.

Tear the bread into a bowl, add the milk, eggs and ricotta and loosely mash. Add the nutmeg, half the sage (chopped) and 25g (scant 1oz) of the Parmesan cheese. Season well. Cover and chill.

Sauté the onion in 1 tbsp of the olive oil until soft and pale gold, then add the garlic and cook for another minute. Set aside. Using the last ½ tbsp of oil, sauté the bacon until golden all over.

Butter a pie dish and put half the bread and milk mixture into it. Add half the squash, all the mozzarella and half the bacon and onions. Ladle on the other half of the bread mixture, then the remaining bacon and onions, then the rest of the squash. Sprinkle on the remaining Parmesan cheese. Leave for 30 minutes (this gives a lighter dish).

Preheat the oven to 180°C/350°F/gas mark 4. Put the dish in a roasting tin and add enough boiling water to the tin to come one-third of the way up the sides of the pie dish. Cook for one hour. Fry the remaining whole sage leaves in very hot olive oil for a few seconds – they will turn crispy – and scatter these on top. Serve with a green salad.

roast beetroots with goat's cheese, rye & dill

YOU'LL FIND IT HARD TO BELIEVE, when you look at how much beetroot you have, that it will only feed four or six people, but they do shrink. There are loads of ways you can go with roast beetroots: mix dill with yogurt and spoon it over instead of goat's cheese, followed by fresh grated horseradish; try a dill-scented gremolata; or go to another area of the world entirely and top with thick yogurt, coriander or dill and slivers of preserved lemon. Serve these while still a little warm.

SERVES 4 as a starter, 6 as a side dish

1.2kg (1lb 10oz) mixed beetroots (regular, golden and candy-stripe if you can get them), preferably the size of golf balls
olive oil
100ml (3½fl oz) buttermilk
3 tbsp rapeseed oil
salt and pepper

2 tbsp chopped dill fronds
50g (1¾oz) rye bread or pumpernickel, whizzed into crumbs
225g (8oz) soft goat's cheese, crumbled
handful of seeds (flax or pumpkin), if you have them

Preheat the oven to 200°C/400°F/gas mark 6. Trim the leaves from the beetroots and wash the beetroots thoroughly. Leave the little straggly tips at the base if you can, but they need to be well cleaned. Put into a roasting tin and drizzle generously with olive oil. Toss everything round with your hands, then add about 50ml (2fl oz) of water. Roast until completely tender; it can take 30 minutes, it can take an hour, depending on the size of the beetroots.

Mix the buttermilk with 2 tbsp of the rapeseed oil, the seasoning and dill. When the beetroots are cool enough to handle, peel off the skins, cut in half lengthways and put in a serving dish.

Heat the remaining rapeseed oil in a frying pan and fry the breadcrumbs until crispy and toasty smelling. Drizzle the beetroots with the buttermilk mixture, then scatter the goat's cheese and breadcrumbs on top. Sprinkle over the seeds, if using, then serve.

biberli cacık

You can't get much simpler than this, but the combination of sweet flesh and tart dressing is irresistible. Use regular peppers if you can't find Turkish or Romano (though they're a lovely shape).

Serves 4

8 long Turkish peppers, or Romano peppers if you can't get those
4 tbsp olive oil
salt and pepper
4 small red chillies, deseeded
250g (9oz) Greek yogurt
4 tbsp buttermilk
2 tbsp extra virgin olive oil, plus more to serve
1 garlic clove, crushed
3 tbsp roughly chopped dill fronds
75g (2¾oz) crumbled feta cheese

Preheat the oven to 200°C/400°F/gas mark 6. Put the peppers into a roasting tin and drizzle with the regular olive oil. Season. Roast in the oven for 25–30 minutes, until they are completely tender, adding the chillies halfway through (tuck them in under the peppers).

Meanwhile, mix the yogurt with the buttermilk, extra virgin olive oil and garlic. It should be thin enough to drizzle.

Put the peppers on a serving plate, pouring any cooking juices from the roasting tin over them. Chop the chillies and scatter them on top. Spoon on the yogurt mixture, then sprinkle with the dill and feta cheese. Drizzle with a little bit more extra virgin olive oil and serve.

roast potatoes with chilli, mint & preserved lemon

STARCHY SIDES are the last thing I think about when preparing a meal and I often just stick little waxy potatoes tossed in olive oil into a hot oven. It's good to have a range of ideas for flavouring them. These are so good I could eat them on their own, but they're also great with any meat (or other vegetable dishes) inspired by the Middle East. You could add some pitted, chopped green olives just before the end of cooking.

SERVES 6 as a side dish
1½ preserved lemons
1kg (2lb 4oz) waxy baby potatoes
4 tbsp olive oil
salt and pepper
½ tsp chilli flakes
3 garlic cloves, finely chopped
about 20 mint leaves, torn

Preheat the oven to 200°C/400°F/gas mark 6.

Remove the flesh from the preserved lemons (discard it) and cut the rind into slivers. Set aside.

The potatoes should be about the size of a walnut (unshelled). If they're larger, then halve them. Put these into a gratin dish, or a small roasting tin, where they can lie in a single layer. Pour on 3 tbsp of the olive oil, season and toss the potatoes round in the oil to get properly coated.

Roast them in the oven for 30 minutes, tossing the chilli flakes in after 15 minutes. The potatoes should be tender right through. Using the last 1 tbsp of olive oil, gently fry the garlic until pale gold. Toss into the potatoes, mixing well, followed by the mint and the preserved lemon rind.

baby potatoes with watercress & garlic cream

POTATOES GET OVERLOOKED, but you can make them special with very little effort. This is most definitely not a salad; the watercress will wilt a little in the heat of the potatoes. It's a good mixture of temperatures and an excellent side dish for so many things: plain roast lamb or chops, chicken or fish.

SERVES 8 as a side dish
1kg (2lb 4oz) baby potatoes
15g (½oz) unsalted butter
squeeze of lemon juice
salt and pepper
250g (9oz) half-fat crème fraîche (half-fat just has a good texture for this)
1 small garlic clove, crushed
75g (2¾oz) watercress, coarse stalks removed
75g (2¾oz) radishes, sliced very thinly, ideally a mixture of pink and purple

Boil the potatoes until tender, then slice roughly and toss in a serving dish with the butter and lemon juice. Season well.

Mix the crème fraîche with the garlic and season. Add the watercress to the potatoes (it will wilt a little, but that's good) and scatter with radishes. Spoon over some of the crème fraîche and offer the rest in a bowl at the table.

roast aubergines with crushed walnuts & anchovies

GOOD WITH ROAST LAMB, or with a range of vegetable dishes served as a main course. You can roast aubergines like this – scoring the flesh makes all the difference – and serve them with things that take less effort. Try a chickpea purée (see page 89), or have a look at the quick sauces and relishes spread (see pages 152–153). Aubergines are so meaty – really satisfying – and go with such a range of flavours.

SERVES 6 as a side dish, 4 as a main course with other vegetables
8 aubergines
olive oil
sea salt flakes and pepper
1 fat garlic clove, chopped
100g (3½oz) walnut pieces
5 anchovies, drained of oil and chopped
5 tbsp extra virgin olive oil
2 tbsp lemon juice, or to taste
1 tsp white balsamic vinegar
3 tbsp finely chopped parsley leaves

Preheat the oven to 190°C/375°F/gas mark 5. Halve the aubergines lengthways. Make a criss-cross pattern on the cut sides, without cutting through, to help heat penetrate. Put into a roasting tin where they can lie in a single layer and paint with regular olive oil. Season. Roast for 25 minutes.

Grind the garlic and a pinch of salt to a paste in a mortar; salt flakes act as an abrasive. Add the walnuts and anchovies and pound until you have a mixture that is part-puréed and part-chunky. Stir in the extra virgin olive oil, lemon juice, vinegar, pepper and the parsley.

Take the aubergines out of the oven, turn them, then return to the oven for 10 minutes. Transfer to a platter, cut sides up, and spoon on the walnut and anchovy mixture.

fragrant sichuan aubergines

THIS IS BASED ON a glorious Sichuan dish in which the aubergine is deep-fried… but I don't trust myself to deep-fry when I'm in a hurry, so I've changed it. If you don't have Chinese black vinegar, use balsamic. The chilli bean paste can be found in some large supermarkets, Asian shops or online (I've also used Korean chilli paste when stuck, it's not Sichuan but it's still damned good). This is thickened with potato flour, but I sometimes leave it out as the sauce can be quite thick enough.

SERVES 4 as a side dish

4 aubergines
4 tbsp groundnut oil
generous 1½ tbsp Sichuan chilli bean paste
  (douban jiang)
2cm (¾in) root ginger, peeled and grated
1 red chilli, deseeded and shredded
4 garlic cloves, very finely chopped
100ml (3½fl oz) chicken stock or water

1½ tsp caster sugar
2 tsp soy sauce
salt and pepper
¾ tsp potato flour
2 tsp Chinese black vinegar
4 spring onions, trimmed and cut into
  5cm (2in) lengths
white sesame seeds

Take the tops off the aubergines. Cut each into three sections, then cut each section into thick batons. Heat 1½ tbsp of the oil in a wok and, over a high heat, cook half the aubergines until they're well-coloured and soft. Remove and set aside. Repeat to cook the rest of the aubergines. Set aside.

Heat the last 1 tbsp of oil in the wok and add the chilli paste. Cook for 20 seconds, then add the ginger, chilli and garlic. Cook for 30 seconds, then add the stock or water, sugar, soy sauce and seasoning. When the mixture comes to a simmer, return the aubergines to the wok and cook for a couple of minutes until they absorb the sauce. Mix the potato flour with 1 tbsp cold water until smooth.

Add the vinegar, spring onions and potato flour mixture to the wok and cook for 30 seconds or so. Taste for seasoning. Sprinkle with sesame seeds and serve immediately with rice.

roast aubergines with tomatoes & saffron cream

IT MIGHT SEEM ODD to mix aubergines – a very Mediterranean vegetable – with cream, but it works here, making a truly luscious dish that is soft and rich and luxurious. Serve this as it is, or scatter shaved Parmesan on top, it depends what else you are offering. It's very good indeed with roast lamb but you can increase the quantities and serve it as a main course, too. Leave the saffron to soak for a good 30 minutes before you use it to develop a much better colour and flavour.

SERVES 6 as a side dish

very generous pinch of saffron stamens
3 aubergines
extra virgin olive oil
6 sprigs of tomatoes on the vine (4–5 tomatoes on each)
salt and pepper
15g (½oz) unsalted butter

2 shallots or ¼ onion
150ml (5fl oz) dry white wine or dry vermouth
500ml (18fl oz) strong chicken or vegetable stock
150ml (5fl oz) double cream
lemon juice, to taste

Put the saffron in a cup and stir in 50ml (2fl oz) of boiling water. Set aside for 30 minutes.

Preheat the oven to 190°C/375°F/gas mark 5. Halve the aubergines lengthways. Cut a cross-hatch pattern on the cut sides, without cutting through (this helps heat penetrate so they roast more quickly). Put into a roasting tin where they and the tomatoes can lie in a single layer. Paint the aubergines with olive oil and drizzle some more on the tomatoes. Season. Roast for 30 minutes.

Melt the butter in a saucepan and cook the shallots until soft but not coloured. Add the wine and boil to reduce to about 50ml (2fl oz). Add the saffron water and stock and boil until reduced by two-thirds. Add the cream and bring to the boil. Season and boil until the sauce can coat the back of a spoon. Strain to remove the shallots. Add a little lemon juice and check the seasoning.

Take the vegetables out of the oven, turn the aubergines over, then roast for a final 10 minutes. Transfer to a warm platter or broad shallow bowl (aubergines cut sides up) and spoon over some of the cream. Serve the rest of the cream on the side.

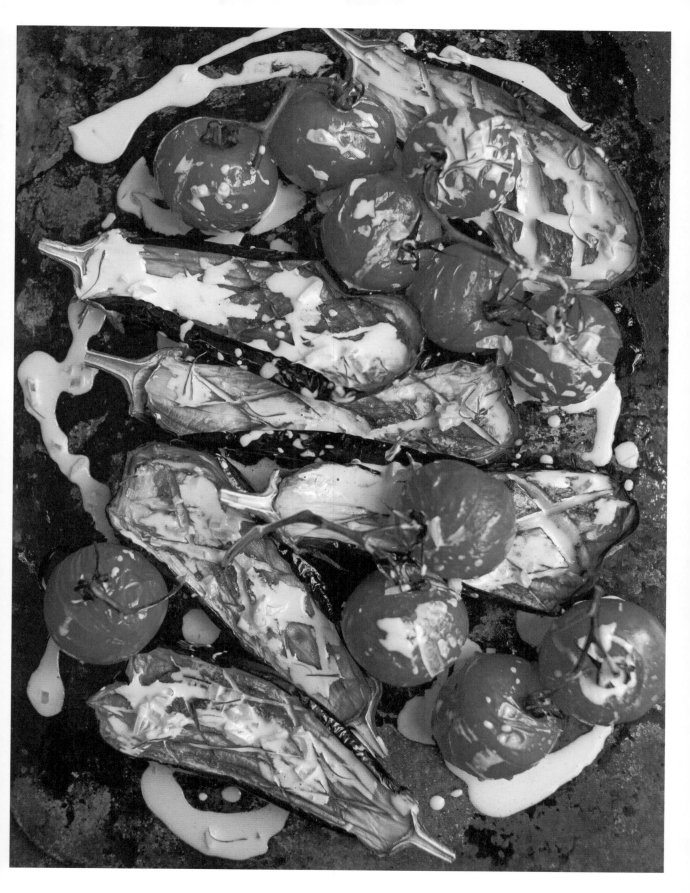

FRUIT
PUDDINGS

pears baked with lemon, bay & marsala

Elegant – even if it's rustic – subtle, autumnal. The bay makes all the difference.

Serves 6
6 fat, just-ripe pears (preferably William)
600ml (1 pint) Marsala
juice of 1 unwaxed lemon, plus the zest of ½, removed in broad strips
6 bay leaves
125g (4½oz) soft light brown sugar

Preheat the oven to 190°C/375°F/gas mark 5.

Halve the pears lengthways. Lay them, cut sides up, in a single layer in a shallow ovenproof dish. The dish should just hold the pears, without lots of room around, otherwise the Marsala will just evaporate. I don't core or peel the pears. If they have stalks leave those on, too.

Pour on the Marsala and lemon juice with 100ml (3½fl oz) of water, tuck the lemon zest under the fruit and add the bay leaves. Sprinkle 100g (3½oz) of the sugar on top of the pears and around them. Bake for 40–45 minutes, or until the pears are tender and starting to wrinkle at the edges. From time to time during cooking, spoon the juices over the top of the pears. Add the remaining 25g (scant 1oz) of sugar towards the end of cooking time. You should have a glossy brown sweet sauce around the pears but, if it looks as if it is toffee-ish and thick, add a little more water. Put the pears in a serving dish, or leave them in the dish in which they've been cooked.

Serve with crème fraîche. You could offer hazelnut or almond biscuits on the side.

roast apple &
maple eton mess

A BIT OF OLD ENGLAND with a big dollop of New England. Have the various components ready, but don't assemble this until you're about to serve or the meringues turn mushy.

SERVES 6

700g (1lb 9oz) Bramley apples, peeled, cored and halved

35g (1¼oz) soft light brown sugar

5 tbsp maple syrup, plus more to serve

30g (1oz) hazelnuts

250ml (9fl oz) whipping cream

75g (2¾oz) Greek yogurt

120g (4¼oz) meringue, roughly broken up

Preheat the oven to 200°C/400°F/gas mark 6. Put the apples into a roasting tin and sprinkle with the sugar. Pour on about 50ml (2fl oz) of water. Roast for 15–20 minutes, or until the fruit is completely tender. Pour on 3 tbsp of the maple syrup and leave to cool. Tip the hazelnuts into a dry frying pan, place over a medium heat and toast until they smell aromatic. Remove and roughly chop.

Break the apples up roughly using a fork; you still want texture. Whip the cream until it holds its shape, then stir in the yogurt and the remaining 2 tbsp of maple syrup.

Layer the apples, cream, hazelnuts and meringue in glasses, drizzling on maple syrup as you go. Finish with a layer of cream and top with a drizzle of maple syrup and some hazelnuts.

roast apricot & orange blossom fool

THE FLAVOUR of roast apricots is incredibly intense and honeyed, so it can easily cope with being 'softened' by cream. Serve with amaretti or *langues de chat* biscuits.

SERVES 8

800g (1lb 12oz) apricots, halved and pitted
75ml (2½fl oz) white wine or water
1 tsp vanilla extract
115g (4oz) granulated sugar
300ml (½ pint) double cream
4 tbsp Greek yogurt
5 tbsp orange blossom honey, or to taste, plus more to serve
3 tsp orange flower water, or to taste
toasted almond flakes, to serve

Preheat the oven to 190°C/375°F/gas mark 5. Put the apricots in a gratin dish, cut sides up, in which they can lie in a single layer. Mix the wine or water with the vanilla in a small bowl and pour it over the fruit, then sprinkle evenly with the sugar.

Roast in the oven for 30–45 minutes (it depends how ripe the fruit is), or until completely soft. Leave until cold. Remove some of the best looking apricot halves to put on top of each serving. Purée the rest of the fruit and all its juice (there won't be much) in a food processor.

Whip the cream – don't let it get too stiff – then stir in the yogurt, honey and flower water. Combine with the apricot purée, but don't mix it so much that you lose the bright orange of the apricots; leave the fool slightly marbled. Taste for sweetness and to check if you want to add more flower water.

Spoon into glasses or bowls. Add an apricot half to each, if you want, drizzle with a little more honey – depending how sweet you found it – then sprinkle with toasted almonds to serve.

summer berries
in mint julep syrup

BERRIES, BOURBON, MINT. What's not to like? Make sure the
syrup is good and cold.

SERVES 6–8
250ml (9fl oz) bourbon
200g (7oz) granulated sugar, or to taste
juice of 4 limes, or to taste
about 40 mint leaves, plus more sprigs of mint to serve
900g (2lb) mixed berries: strawberries, blueberries, raspberries and redcurrants

Put 200ml (7fl oz) of the bourbon into a pan with the sugar and half the lime juice. Pour in
150ml (5fl oz) of water and bring to the boil, stirring a little to help the sugar dissolve. Add half
the mint leaves and boil until reduced by half. Remove from the heat and pour in the remaining
lime juice and bourbon. Taste – you may want more sugar or a little more lime – then leave to
cool. Strain to remove the mint, then chill.

Hull the strawberries and cut into slices about the thickness of a £1 coin. Put into a bowl with
the rest of the berries and currants and pour over the chilled syrup and the remaining mint
leaves. Put in the fridge for about 30 minutes, any longer and the fruit gets too soft. Serve with
whipped cream, adding a sprig of mint to each serving.

peaches in peach
tea with rosemary

HERBAL AND INTENSELY PEACHY. You could use lavender instead
of rosemary, if you prefer.

SERVES 6
2 peach tea bags (or another fruit tea, berry or apple would work)
125g (4½oz) granulated sugar
3 sprigs of rosemary, plus more to serve
juice of 2 lemons, plus 2 broad strips of unwaxed lemon zest
6 peaches, halved and pitted

Put the tea bags into a jug with 1 litre (1¾ pints) of boiling water and leave to brew for about
seven minutes. Discard the tea bags and pour the tea into a saucepan large enough to take
all the peaches in a single layer. Add the sugar and stir to dissolve. Add the rosemary, lemon
juice and zest and peaches. Bring to a simmer and gently poach the peaches until they are
tender. This will take 12–25 minutes, depending how ripe your peaches are. Keep checking,
sticking the tip of a sharp knife into the hollow where the peach stones were.

Scoop out the peaches with a slotted spoon and set them on a dish so that they are not
touching (if you pile them on top of each other they will continue to cook and soften).

Remove the lemon zest and one of the sprigs of rosemary from the poaching liquid, then
bring it to the boil and cook until the liquid is reduced to a syrup; you should have about
250ml (9fl oz) of liquid. Set aside to cool completely, leaving the rosemary in the syrup.

Put the peaches into a serving dish and strain over the syrup. Add a few fresh sprigs of
rosemary to serve.

summer fruit
& almond cake

A LOVELY CAKE for August or September, when fruit is abundant. You
can use a different fruit mixture – peaches, blackberries and figs would
be good, too – as long as the stone fruit is ripe.

SERVES 8

For the cake
110g (4oz) unsalted butter, softened, plus more
    for the tin
125g (4½oz) caster sugar
2 large eggs, lightly beaten
1 tsp vanilla extract
½ tsp almond extract
185g (6½oz) plain flour
¾ tsp baking powder
100g (3½oz) sour cream
100g (3½oz) marzipan, broken into little chunks
pinch of salt

For the fruit
2 ripe nectarines, halved, pitted and sliced
1 large or 2 smaller unripe plums, halved,
    pitted and sliced
60g (2¼oz) raspberries
3 tbsp caster sugar
a little icing sugar, to dust

Preheat the oven to 190°C/375°F/gas mark 5. Butter a 20cm (8in) springform cake tin and line it
with greaseproof paper.

Put all the ingredients for the cake into a food processor and whizz until smooth. Scrape the
batter into the prepared tin.

Toss the fruit with the caster sugar and lay the pieces, higgledy-piddledy, on top of the batter.

Bake for 1½ hours. The cake is ready when a skewer inserted into the middle comes out clean
(although the marzipan does make it hard to judge this cake, which is rich and moist). Leave to
cool in the tin, then carefully remove the ring and the base. Peel off the paper and slide the cake
on to a plate. Dust lightly with icing sugar to serve.

berries & melon in elderflower syrup

THE ELDERFLOWER SYRUP here is very useful: you can poach apricots or little halved apples in it, or pour it on to sliced ripe peaches or mangoes.

SERVES 6

400ml (14fl oz) white wine
175g (6oz) granulated sugar
juice of 1 lemon, plus 2 broad strips of unwaxed lemon zest
2 tbsp elderflower cordial, or to taste (they vary considerably in strength)
½ Chanterais or Ogen melon
200g (7oz) strawberries, hulled, halved or quartered (leave very small berries whole)
200g (7oz) raspberries

Mix the wine, sugar, lemon juice and zest together with 200ml (7fl oz) of water in a saucepan and slowly bring to the boil, stirring a little to help the sugar dissolve. Boil for seven minutes. Take it off the heat and add the cordial, then leave to cool completely. You should have a light syrup. Strain.

Remove the seeds from the melon and cut the fruit into slices. Remove the skin from each slice and place into a broad, shallow bowl with the strawberries and raspberries. Pour over the cooled syrup. Chill briefly (if you leave the fruit in the syrup for too long the fruit gets unpleasantly soft), or serve at room temperature with whipped cream or crème fraîche.

baked plums in sloe gin

SIMPLICITY ITSELF. If you have damson gin lying around, that
works well, too. And pears are good instead of plums.

SERVES 4
12 plums, halved and pitted
100ml (3½fl oz) sloe gin, plus 1½ tbsp to serve
juice of 1 orange, plus 2 broad strips of orange zest
5 juniper berries, crushed
50g (1¾oz) soft light brown sugar

Preheat the oven to 200°C/400°F/gas mark 6.

Put the plums into a roasting tin in which they can lie snugly in a single layer, cut sides up. Mix
the gin and orange juice and pour it over the fruit. Tuck the orange zest and juniper berries in
under the fruit. Sprinkle with the sugar and bake for 20 minutes, or until tender.

Using a slotted spoon, lift the plums out of the roasting tin and into a serving dish to cool
(don't pile them on top of each other, otherwise they continue to cook and can get too soft).

Put the roasting tin over a high heat and bring the juices to the boil. Cook until they're reduced
and slightly syrupy looking. Be careful, though: if you've used a tin where there's quite a lot of
room round the fruit, the juices will have evaporated more and may already be thick enough.
They will thicken more as they cool. Chill, then pour over the plums with the extra 1½ tbsp sloe
gin, just to boost the booziness.

sherry-roasted pear & chocolate sundaes

PEARS, SHERRY, CHOCOLATE, this is a heady and wonderful mixture. You don't have to serve it in sundae glasses, of course, just use what you have. The important thing is to be generous. And be careful not to overheat the chocolate sauce; go slowly and keep everything warm, not hot, and all will be well.

SERVES 8

8 pears, under-ripe, halved and cored
500ml (18fl oz) sweet sherry
juice of 1 lemon
40g (1½oz) soft dark brown sugar
200g (7oz) good-quality dark chocolate (70% cocoa solids), broken into pieces
100ml (3½fl oz) whole milk
50ml (2fl oz) double cream
45g (1½oz) caster sugar, plus 1½ tbsp
25g (scant 1oz) unsalted butter
200ml (7fl oz) whipping cream
1 tsp vanilla extract
tub of vanilla ice cream
45g (1¾oz) hazelnuts, halved and toasted (see page 281)

Preheat the oven to 190°C/375°F/gas mark 5. Lay the pears, cut sides up, in a single layer in a shallow ovenproof dish. Pour on the sherry, lemon juice and 80ml (2½fl oz) of water. Sprinkle the brown sugar on the pears and bake for 40–45 minutes, or until tender. Leave to cool.

Put the chocolate in a heatproof bowl and melt over a pan of simmering water. Separately heat the milk, double cream and 45g (1½oz) of caster sugar, stirring to help the sugar melt. Slowly whisk the milk into the melted chocolate; at first it will look as though it won't blend in, but keep beating and it comes together. Whisk in the butter until it melts. Leave to cool a little; it is good if the sauce is warm. Whip the whipping cream and vanilla with the 1½ tbsp caster sugar.

Assemble the sundaes, in sundae glasses or bowls, arranging the pears, ice cream, nuts and chocolate sauce. Top with whipped cream, a final drizzle of chocolate sauce and more hazelnuts.

hot cherries with grappa & ice cream

I ATE THIS in a restaurant in Norcia in Umbria. I travelled most of the day to get there because Claudia Roden, writing in *The Observer* newspaper, had recommended it. It was the most modest place and the food – a tomato and basil salad, lamb chops *scottadito* with fried potatoes, sausages with lentils, and this pudding – has stayed with me. It was a perfect meal. The owners had no idea that Claudia had recommended them and were so thrilled that they thanked us with more grappa than we could drink. (And ran around Norcia on a Sunday night trying to find a photocopier to copy Claudia's piece. I left it with them.) This is a last-minute pudding and some people hate serving those – they like to have everything sorted before their friends arrive – but it takes very little time and there's something lovely about taking warm cherries to the table in a frying pan.

SERVES 4
25g (scant 1oz) unsalted butter
450g (1lb) pitted cherries (I like to tear them rather than cut them to remove the stones)
100g (3½oz) caster sugar
juice of ½ lemon
3–4 tbsp grappa
vanilla ice cream, to serve

Melt the butter in a large frying pan, then add the cherries and any juices that came out of them when you were pitting them. Toss them around over a medium heat, adding the sugar and stirring gently to help it dissolve. Add the lemon juice. Keep tossing the cherries and cooking until they have a thickish syrup around them.

Add the grappa (you can now flambé the cherries if you want, but it's not necessary) and you're done. Take to the table and serve cold ice cream with the hot cherries.

white nectarines & raspberries in rosé

A REALLY ELEGANT PUDDING. Peaches can be used instead, but I like the slight tartness of nectarines, and the fragrance of the white-fleshed fruits.

SERVES 6

600ml (1 pint) rosé wine
225g (8oz) granulated sugar, plus 25g (scant 1oz)
2 strips of unwaxed lemon zest, plus the juice of ½ lemon
6 white nectarines or peaches, halved and pitted
175g (6oz) raspberries

Put the wine, sugar, lemon zest and juice in a pan big enough to hold the nectarines, preferably in a single layer. Bring to the boil, stirring to help the sugar dissolve, then reduce the heat. Add the nectarines and poach gently, turning every so often, until they are just tender: start checking after eight minutes, then keep checking, as they can get soft quite suddenly. Remove the fruit as it's ready and allow to cool lying in a single layer, then boil the poaching liquid until it is reduced and slightly syrupy. You want to end up with 250–300ml (9–10fl oz). Set aside until cold; the liquid will thicken more as it cools.

Carefully remove the skins from the nectarines, they should just slip off. Pour the cold syrup over the nectarines and chill.

Just before serving, gently stir in the raspberries, being careful not to break them up.

rhubarb & raspberry crumble cake

VERY MOIST, this makes as good a pudding as it does a teatime cake.

SERVES 8

For the cake
125g (4½oz) unsalted butter, more for the tin
125g (4½oz) caster sugar, plus 5 tbsp more
   for the fruit
3 large eggs, lightly beaten
2 tsp vanilla extract
125g (4½oz) self-raising flour
2 tbsp milk (optional)
675g (1lb 8oz) rhubarb, trimmed and cut into
   2.5cm (1in) lengths
100g (3½oz) raspberries
icing sugar, to dust

For the crumble
170g (6oz) plain flour
100g (3½oz) cold unsalted butter, cubed
100g (3½oz) golden caster sugar
100g (3½oz) flaked almonds

Preheat the oven to 180°C/350°F/gas mark 4. Butter a 23cm (9in) springform tin.

Beat the butter and the 125g (4½oz) sugar together until pale and fluffy. Add the eggs a little at a time, beating well after each addition, then add the vanilla. If the mixture starts to curdle, add 1 tbsp of the flour. Fold in the remaining flour, then add enough milk to give the batter a reluctant dropping consistency. Scrape into the prepared tin.

Toss the rhubarb and raspberries with the 5 tbsp of caster sugar and spread it over the top of the cake batter. For the crumble, rub the flour and butter together with your fingers until the mixture resembles breadcrumbs. Stir in the sugar and almonds and scatter over the fruit.

Bake for one hour 20 minutes. The top should be golden and a skewer inserted into the middle of the cake should come out clean. Leave to cool in the tin, then carefully remove the ring and base. Dust with icing sugar to serve.

apricot & amaretti crostata

LIKE FREE-FORM TARTS, crostatas are very forgiving. If the pastry tears as you are shaping it or crimping the edges, just patch it up. You can use ground almonds, walnuts or hazelnuts instead of the amaretti (and leave out the liqueur, too), or make this tart with peaches or plums instead.

SERVES 8–10

280g (10oz) plain flour, plus more to dust

150g (5½oz) unsalted butter, chilled and cut into rough cubes

75g (2¾oz) icing sugar, plus more to serve

1 egg yolk

1 tbsp double cream

100g (3½oz) amaretti biscuits, crushed

2 tbsp granulated sugar

600g (1lb 5oz) apricots, pitted and quartered (neither over-ripe nor very under-ripe)

2 tbsp lemon juice

2 tbsp amaretto liqueur (optional)

Put the flour, butter and icing sugar into a food processor and whizz until you have a breadcrumb-like mixture. Add the egg yolk and cream and whizz again. It should come together into a ball. If it doesn't, add a couple of tsp of very cold water and whizz again. Wrap in cling film and put in the fridge to rest for an hour; longer is fine, too.

When ready to bake, preheat the oven to 190°C/375°F/gas mark 5. Roll out the pastry on a lightly floured piece of baking parchment into a circle, about 32cm (13in) across. Mix the crushed amaretti with half the granulated sugar. Leaving a 3.5cm (1½in) border all the way round, sprinkle on the amaretti mixture. Lay the apricots on top in a higgledy-piggledy fashion. Sprinkle on the rest of the sugar followed by the lemon juice and the liqueur, if using. Pull the edges of the pastry up around and over the edges of the fruit and pinch it slightly all the way round, or just pinch it up to make a higher rim. Patch it up if it breaks. Slide, still on its baking parchment, on to a baking sheet. Bake for 35 minutes. If the pastry gets too dark, cover it with foil. The fruit should be tender and slightly singed in parts. Leave to cool a little and sift over icing sugar just before serving.

melon granita

THERE AREN'T MANY PUDDINGS EASIER to make than a granita.
You just need a fork and a freezer. Melon granita should be strongly
perfumed – use perfectly ripe melons, Charentais is the best variety
for this – and a gorgeous colour, too. The last time I made this was
in the middle of a heatwave. I forgot about it until one night when
I was testing recipes very late and had the oven on. I suddenly
remembered this was stashed away in the freezer and ate a bowl of it,
in the garden, after midnight, the granita melting almost faster than
I could eat it. It was bliss.

SERVES 6

250g (9oz) caster sugar
2 Charentais melons
juice of 3 limes, or to taste

Bring 250ml (9fl oz) of water to the boil, then take it off the heat and add the sugar. Stir until
the sugar has dissolved, then set aside to cool.

It's important to capture every bit of juice from the melons, so cut them on a board set on
a tray with a lip all the way round. Halve the melons and remove the seeds. Scoop the flesh
out with a spoon into a bowl. Set a sieve over the bowl and put all the juice that's collected
in the tray into the sieve, along with the seeds and the fibres round them. Press lightly to
extract more juice.

Whizz the melon flesh and all the juice you've collected in a food processor. Push it through
a sieve. Combine this purée with the sugar syrup and the juice of 1–2 limes. Taste. You'll
probably need the juice of the other lime, but you don't want to spoil the delicate taste of the
melon by going too far, so use your judgement.

Put into a shallow container and place in the freezer. Fork through the mixture every so
often as it is freezing, to create icy shards. Serve just as it is, in little chilled glasses.

roast apple, blackberry & whiskey trifles

No CUSTARD, I know, but these qualify as little trifles in my book. You could add a layer of custard if you wanted to, though; a good bought tub of fresh custard is fine. Double the quantities if you want to make a single trifle in a big bowl.

SERVES 4

525g (1lb 3oz) Bramley apples, peeled, cored and quartered

35g (1¼oz) soft light brown sugar, plus 1½ tbsp for the cream

about 36 blackberries

1½ tbsp caster sugar

125ml (4fl oz) apple juice

50g (1¾oz) granulated sugar

4 tbsp whiskey, or to taste

250ml (9fl oz) double cream

16 sponge fingers

25g (scant 1oz) halved hazelnuts, toasted (see page 281)

Preheat the oven to 200°C/400°F/gas mark 6. Put the apples into a roasting tin and sprinkle with the 35g (1¼oz) of soft light brown sugar. Roast in the oven until the apples are completely tender, about 30 minutes. They will burst and look quite messy, but that's okay. Put them, and their juices, into a bowl and mash with a fork. Leave to cool.

Set aside some blackberries for decoration and toss the rest in a bowl with the caster sugar. Put the juice in a small pan with the granulated sugar and bring to the boil, stirring to dissolve the sugar. Leave to cool, then add 2 tbsp of the whiskey. Whip the cream and stir in the remaining 1½ tbsp soft light brown sugar and 2 tbsp of whiskey. Get four glasses, cups or bowls ready.

Halve the sponge fingers and dip half of them into the apple syrup. Keep them there until they are really soggy but haven't fallen apart, then lay them in the glasses. Add a layer of apple purée, then some cream, then soak the other half of the sponge fingers in syrup and lay them on top.

Divide the blackberries that have been sitting in sugar between the four glasses. Spoon some of the apple syrup over each serving, shaking it to help it run down into the layers. Top with more cream and scatter with hazelnuts and the reserved blackberries.

baked apples with marmalade & southern comfort cream

IF YOU THINK Southern Comfort tastes like cough mixture (or too much like adolescence) then use whiskey, bourbon, apple brandy or a little Cointreau instead. Everyone likes a baked apple, but they do need something to make them a little special.

SERVES 8

For the apples
130g (4¾oz) sultanas and raisins
300ml (½ pint) orange juice
finely grated zest of 1 orange
8 eating apples, preferably with stalks
75g (2¾oz) roughly chopped hazelnuts or
    walnuts, lightly toasted (see page 281)
150g (5½oz) soft light brown sugar

For the marmalade cream
300ml (½ pint) double cream
125g (4½oz) marmalade, not too firm-set
icing sugar, to taste
1½ tbsp Southern Comfort, or to taste

Put the dried fruit in a saucepan with half the orange juice and bring to the boil. Reduce the heat and simmer for about five minutes, then take the pan off the heat, add the zest and leave the fruit for about 30 minutes to plump up. Preheat the oven to 180°C/350°F/gas mark 4.

Slice the top off each apple to make a lid about 5cm (2in) across, then core the rest of each fruit. Remove a little of the flesh around the core, too, so there is room for the stuffing. Put them in an ovenproof dish. Mix the plumped-up dried fruit with the nuts and brown sugar. Spoon the stuffing into each apple, sprinkling leftovers around the dish, and put the apple lids on. Pour on the remaining orange juice. Bake for 30–40 minutes, or until completely tender, spooning any juices over every so often (keep an eye on them, as they get to bursting stage very suddenly).

Whip the cream until it just holds its shape, then beat in the marmalade until it has broken down. Add the icing sugar (you won't need much) and Southern Comfort, or whatever booze you are using. Serve the apples warm, with their cooking juices and the cream.

marmalade baked fruit with boozy orange cream

SO EASY. Use a marmalade with fine shreds if you can. It's important that both the pears and the plums are slightly under-ripe, otherwise they will over-cook and fall apart before the apples are tender.

SERVES 6

For the fruit
2 pears (long and skinny, such as Conference), slightly under-ripe
juice of 2 lemons
2 apples
6 slightly under-ripe plums, halved and pitted
finely grated zest of 1 orange
125g (4½oz) orange marmalade

1½ tbsp golden syrup
2 tbsp sherry or whiskey

For the cream
200ml (7fl oz) whipping cream
finely grated zest of ½ orange
1 tbsp soft dark brown sugar
Cointreau, to taste

Preheat the oven to 190°C/375°F/gas mark 5.

Quarter the pears lengthways and core the pieces. You don't need to peel them. Put them in a large ovenproof dish from which you can serve (or a roasting tin is fine, you can transfer them to a serving dish later). Immediately pour the lemon juice on to the pears. The bits of fruit (including the apples and plums) shouldn't be piled on top of each other, they should lie in a single layer. Halve and core the apples and cut each half into four wedges. Add to the pears followed by the plums and the orange zest. Mix the fruit round with your hands to ensure it gets covered in juice.

Stir together the marmalade, syrup and alcohol, using the back of a spoon to break the marmalade down. Spoon this all over the fruit and bake for 40 minutes, or until the fruit is tender and slightly caramelized, basting with the cooking juices every so often.

To make the cream, whip it until it is beginning to thicken, then add the zest and sugar. Whip again until it is holding its shape well, then gradually add the Cointreau. Serve the fruit warm or at room temperature, with the cream on the side.

st clements & rosemary posset with blackberries

POSSET IS A WONDER. All you do is heat cream, add citrus juice and leave to cool… and yet you end up with a silky, rich dessert. You can top this with any fruit – blueberries, poached rhubarb, raspberries – as long as it's quite tart.

SERVES 6
500ml (18fl oz) double cream
1 sprig of rosemary
150g (5½oz) caster sugar
juice of 1 lemon and ½ orange
blackberries, to serve

Put the cream, rosemary and sugar into a heavy-based saucepan and slowly bring to the boil, stirring from time to time to help the sugar dissolve. Take it off the heat and leave to infuse for 30 minutes. Remove the rosemary, place back over the heat, bring to the boil, then reduce the heat slightly and let the cream bubble away for three minutes: you need to watch it like a hawk, in case it boils over.

Pour into a bowl and whisk in the citrus juices. Divide the mixture between six small glasses or cups and allow to cool, then cover and refrigerate. The posset will firm up. It needs to be in the fridge for about three hours.

Just before serving, put some blackberries on top of each posset.

no-hassle puddings

I love planning and cooking puddings, but rarely make anything very complicated. That's less to do with a shortage of time and more to do with the fact that simple puddings are among the best, especially when fruit is good. None of the following sweet endings are remotely taxing.

FRAISES MAM GOZ
A Breton strawberry dish. Heat 150ml (5fl oz) each red wine and water with 100g (3½oz) granulated sugar, stirring a little. Boil for seven minutes. Cool and add a little orange flower water, to taste. Pour over hulled and halved strawberries and leave for 1 hour.

MEL I MATO
A Catalonian way with dried fruit. Serve a mild, creamy goat's cheese with dried fruit, toasted almonds or hazelnuts, a drizzle of thyme honey and a glass of chilled Muscatel.

BERRIES, MERINGUES & CURD CREAM
Mix whipped cream with good-quality orange or lemon curd and the pulp of a few passion fruits. Serve big, shop-bought meringues with the cream spooned over them, scattered with mixed berries.

ROAST BANANA & BROWN SUGAR FOOL

Put 5 really ripe, peeled bananas in an ovenproof dish with the finely grated zest and juice of 2 limes, plenty of soft dark brown sugar and a good slug of dark rum. Bake in a medium oven for about 1 hour. Cool, then mash with 250ml (9fl oz) whipped double cream and some Greek yogurt. Add more rum or sugar to taste and chill before serving.

BAKED PEACHES WITH AMARETTO

Bake halved and pitted ripe peaches, topped with soft brown sugar and splashes of amaretto liqueur, in a hot oven for 30 minutes, or until tender to the point of a knife. Serve with whipped cream mixed with a good slug of amaretto liqueur, then sprinkle the whole thing with crumbled amaretti biscuits.

WHITE NECTARINES WITH MUSCAT

If you can find perfectly ripe white nectarines, nothing is better than this. Halve and pit the nectarines and serve on a platter with whitecurrants (they look like glowing pearls) and glasses of very cold Muscat de Beaumes de Venise.

BLACKBERRIES & CRÈME DE CASSIS

Put blackberries in a bowl – you can mix them with blackcurrants, too – sprinkle with caster sugar and gently stir in a couple of tablespoons of crème de cassis. Serve with a mound of ricotta, crème fraîche or vanilla ice cream.

GRILLED APRICOTS & HONEY

Halve and pit ripe apricots, put them in a gratin dish and drizzle with honey. Put these under a hot grill and cook until bubbling (be careful not to let it go too far). Serve with crème fraîche and chopped pistachio nuts.

PEACH MELBA

Make a raspberry sauce by whizzing 200g (7oz) raspberries with 30g (1oz) icing sugar in a food processor. Push through a sieve, to remove the seeds. Layer perfectly ripe – or poached (see page 296) – peaches in tall glasses with the sauce and scoops of vanilla ice cream.

RASPBERRY-CHOCOLATE SUNDAE

Layer scoops of vanilla ice cream in a tall glass with crumbled, gooey-centred brownies, raspberries and the raspberry sauce above. Finish with softly whipped cream. For a boozy version, add crème de framboise to the sauce.

RASPBERRY & WHISKEY TRIFLE

Put two slices of good sponge cake – spread with raspberry jam – into soup plates and douse with whiskey mixed with a little sugar. Spoon some good bought vanilla custard (I like the Waitrose version) on top, followed by raspberries and sweetened whipped cream.

CHOCOLATE BARK

Melt good-quality dark or white chocolate, then pour on to a greaseproof paper-lined tray. Top white chocolate bark with freeze-dried raspberries, blanched almonds, pistachio nuts and dried rose petals. Top dark chocolate bark with toasted hazelnuts, chopped dried apricots and candied orange; or dried sour cherries and walnuts. Break into shards once set.

OTHER
SWEET
THINGS

sgroppino

I KNOW, I KNOW, barely a recipe and some would argue it's a cocktail rather than a dessert anyway. However you want to classify it, this is a pretty magnificent end to a meal. A sgroppino is a Venetian invention and it should, properly, be shaken and served in a foamy froth, but I like the look of the sorbet floating in the glass and, in any case, the sorbet quickly melts, producing a froth on its own. The pureness of lemon sorbet is very pleasing, but even in Venice they serve different flavours now. Peach or raspberry sorbet are good. And I've seen the odd fresh raspberry added, too.

SERVES 6

6 scoops of really good-quality lemon sorbet
6 glasses of chilled prosecco, only half filled
6 tbsp vodka

Add the sorbet to the half glasses of prosecco carefully, as the wine will froth up. (When it has died down a little, you can top up with more wine.) Add the vodka, too, and serve.

lemon & lavender cake

You can now buy dried edible lavender (Bart Ingredients sells it).
If you want proper icing, use the glacé icing recipe from later in
this chapter (see page 327).

Serves 8
unsalted butter, for the tin
300g (10½oz) granulated sugar
¾ tbsp dried lavender
175g (6oz) plain flour
½ tsp baking powder
½ tsp bicarbonate of soda
¼ tsp salt
2 large eggs, lightly beaten
250g (9oz) Greek yogurt
125ml (4fl oz) mild-flavoured olive oil
finely grated zest of 1 unwaxed lemon, plus 1 tbsp lemon juice
icing sugar, to dust
sprigs of fresh lavender, to serve

Preheat the oven to 180°C/350°F/gas mark 4. Butter a 20cm (8in) diameter, 6cm (2½in) deep cake tin and line the base with baking parchment.

Put the granulated sugar and lavender into a food processor and whizz until the lavender has broken down. Sift the flour, baking powder, bicarbonate of soda and salt together into a bowl. Stir in the lavender sugar. In a jug, mix the eggs with the yogurt and oil. Make a well in the centre of the dry ingredients and gradually stir in the wet ingredients. Add the lemon zest and juice, but don't over-mix. Scrape into the prepared tin.

Bake for 45–50 minutes, or until the cake is coming away from the sides of the tin and a skewer inserted into the middle comes out clean. Turn it out, peel off the paper and set on a wire rack until cold. Dust with icing sugar just before serving and decorate with sprigs of fresh lavender.

bitter flourless chocolate cake with coffee cream

I'VE MADE SO MANY versions of this cake over the years that I could now bake it in my sleep. It's the little black dress of puddings: elegant and timeless. Do it a few times and it will become easy. Serve with a marmalade cream (see page 305) instead of the coffee version, or simply with summer berries and cream, or Hot cherries with grappa (see page 294).

SERVES 8

For the cake
160g (5¾oz) unsalted butter, plus more for the tin
320g (11½oz) good-quality dark chocolate
   (70% cocoa solids), broken into pieces
145g (5¼oz) caster sugar
5 large eggs, separated
40g (1½oz) ground almonds
icing sugar, to dust

For the cream
300ml (½ pint) double cream
½ tbsp instant espresso coffee dissolved
   in ½ tbsp boiling water
2 tbsp whiskey, or to taste
3 tbsp icing sugar, or to taste

Preheat the oven to 180°C/350°F/gas mark 4. Butter a 20cm (8in) springform cake tin.

Put the chocolate, butter and sugar into a heatproof bowl set over a pan of simmering water (the water shouldn't touch the bowl). Melt the mixture, stirring a little. Remove the bowl and leave it to cool for about four minutes. Stir in the egg yolks, one at a time.

Beat the egg whites with electric beaters until they form medium peaks (stiff but with the peaks drooping slightly). Using a big metal spoon, fold the ground almonds into the chocolate mixture along with half the egg whites, then fold in the rest of the whites.

Scrape the batter into the prepared tin and bake for 35 minutes. Cool completely, carefully remove the ring and base and put the cake on a serving plate. It will deflate and crack as it cools. Whip the cream until just holding its shape, then drizzle in the coffee and whiskey, still whipping. Add the icing sugar and taste for sweetness and booziness. Sift icing sugar over the cake and serve with the cream.

roopa's kheer with scented fruits

I CAN'T REALLY write a book without including a few recipes from my friend Roopa Gulati, I love her food so much. She brought this rice dish to my house, but we talked so much that day we never got round to eating it. She wouldn't take it home, but left it in the fridge. I confess I ate it for breakfast for the rest of the week (indulgent, I know). Serve the rice thick, but not stodgy.

SERVES 8

For the kheer
generous pinch of saffron strands
10 cardamom pods
1.4 litres (2½ pints) whole milk, more if needed
225g (8oz) basmati rice
85g (3oz) pistachio nuts, shelled, more to serve
110g (3¾oz) caster sugar, more if needed
½–1 tbsp good-quality rose water
50ml (2fl oz) thick double cream

For the dried fruit
185g (6½oz) caster sugar
2 broad strips of orange zest
150g (5½oz) raisins, or a mixture of dried fruit
    including raisins, chopped apples, sour
    cherries and chopped apricots
juice of ½ lemon or 1 lime
1 tsp rose water, or more to taste

Soak the saffron in 3 tbsp of just-boiled water for at least 30 minutes. Split the cardamom pods, add to the milk in a heavy-based pan and bring to scalding point. Stir in the rice, reduce the heat and simmer for 30–40 minutes, until tender and thick. Stir often; add more milk if needed.

Finely chop the pistachio nuts, or blitz in a food processor. Add the sugar to the rice and stir until dissolved, then stir in the nuts and saffron with its soaking liquid. Leave to cool, then chill. It will get thicker so, if it's already thick, you'll need more milk and possibly more sugar. Stir the rose water into the chilled rice – very gradually in case it is strong – with the cream.

For the dried fruit, heat 200ml (7fl oz) of water with the caster sugar and orange zest, stirring to help the sugar dissolve. When it comes to the boil, take it off the heat and add the fruit. Leave to cool in the syrup. Once it's cold, add the citrus juice and rose water (go easy with the latter).

Spoon into small bowls. Scatter with pistachio nuts to serve and offer the fruit on the side.

espresso loaf cake with burnt butter & coffee icing

THIS IS DENSER THAN REGULAR coffee cake, as it's made by the melt-and-mix method. I use a coffee extract for it, made by Nielsen-Massey. If you can't find it, use Camp Coffee, available in most supermarkets.

SERVES 10

For the cake

225g (8oz) unsalted butter, plus more for the tin

200ml (7fl oz) strong coffee, preferably espresso

150g (5½oz) soft light brown sugar

225g (8oz) golden syrup

2 tsp coffee extract

2 large eggs, lightly beaten

240g (8½oz) plain flour

100g (3½oz) malted brown flour, or wholemeal

pinch of salt

1 tsp bicarbonate of soda

75g (2¾oz) roughly chopped walnuts

For the icing

2 tbsp instant espresso powder

100g (3½oz) unsalted butter

200g (7oz) icing sugar, sifted

2 tbsp toasted walnuts, chopped (see page 112)

Preheat the oven to 170°C/340°F/gas mark 3½. Butter a loaf tin that measures 23 x 12.5 x 7cm (9 x 5 x 2½in) and line the base with baking parchment.

Put the coffee in a pan with the butter, sugar and syrup. Heat gently, without boiling, stirring to dissolve the sugar. Pour into a jug and leave to cool. Whisk in the coffee extract and eggs.

Sift the flours, salt and bicarbonate of soda into a bowl, then add the bran from the sieve. Toss in the walnuts. Make a well in the dry ingredients and slowly pour in the wet mixture, stirring together gradually. Scrape into the prepared tin and bake for one hour 15 minutes. A skewer inserted into the centre should come out clean. Leave to cool in the tin for 10 minutes, then turn out on to a wire rack, peel off the paper and turn the right way up. Allow to cool.

Dissolve the espresso powder in 2 tbsp of boiling water and cool. Melt the butter in a pan, then increase the heat and cook until it has just turned brown and nutty. Leave to cool. Put the butter in a mixer with the icing sugar and beat, gradually adding the coffee. Cover and chill to firm up.

Using a palette knife, spread the icing over the cake. As it's a tea cake, fancy embellishments aren't quite right, but scatter with the toasted chopped walnuts.

lemon & ricotta cake

VERY MOIST because of the ricotta, though for the same reason it doesn't keep fantastically well. Try to eat it within a day of being made. It's the perfect cake with which to welcome spring.

SERVES 8

175g (6oz) unsalted butter, softened, plus more for the tin
175g (6oz) golden caster sugar
finely grated zest of 4 unwaxed lemons, plus the juice of 3
3 large eggs, separated, yolks lightly beaten
250g (9oz) fresh ricotta (if possible, not UHT stuff), drained in a sieve
100g (3½oz) self-raising flour, sifted
25g (scant 1oz) ground almonds, freshly ground if possible
1 tsp baking powder
icing sugar, to serve

Preheat the oven to 180°C/350°F/gas mark 4. Butter a 20cm (8in) springform cake tin.

Beat the butter and sugar together in an electric mixer until pale and fluffy, then beat in the zest. Gradually add the egg yolks, beating well after each addition. Drain off any liquid that is in the ricotta (there's usually a little bit). Stir the drained ricotta into the batter.

Beat the egg whites separately until they form medium peaks. Stir the lemon juice into the batter, then fold in the flour, almonds and baking powder. Fold two big spoons of the beaten egg whites into the batter to loosen it, then fold in the rest. Scrape the batter into the prepared tin. Put it in the oven and bake for 45–50 minutes. A skewer inserted into the middle of the cake should come out clean once it's cooked. It is a very moist cake because of the ricotta and doesn't have the texture of a regular cake, such as a Victoria sponge.

Carefully remove the springform ring from around the cake and let it cool. This is lovely just slightly warm, but you can let it cool completely. Dust with icing sugar and serve with berries and crème fraîche or whipped cream.

raisin, lemon & marsala bread & butter pudding

BREAD AND BUTTER PUDDING – and limitless riffs on it – has been my 'go-to' dessert for the last 20 years. This has a Sicilian spin. Make it twice and you won't have to think about it and can adapt it at will. The unchangeable elements are the quantities of milk, cream, eggs, sugar, butter and bread. Put it in the oven as soon as your guests arrive.

SERVES 6

100g (3½oz) raisins
100ml (3½fl oz) Marsala, plus more if needed
300ml (½ pint) whole milk
300ml (½ pint) double cream
2 broad strips of unwaxed lemon zest,
    plus finely grated zest of ½ lemon
150g (5½oz) caster sugar

pinch of salt
3 large eggs, plus 1 egg yolk
½ tsp vanilla extract
50g (1¾oz) unsalted butter
about 250g (9oz) sweet bread, such as
    challah or brioche, sliced
icing sugar, to dust

Put the raisins into a small saucepan and add the Marsala. Bring to just under the boil, then take off the heat and leave to plump up for 30 minutes.

Bring the milk, cream, broad strips of zest, 100g (3½oz) of the sugar and the salt to the boil in a heavy-based pan. Remove from the heat. Beat the egg whites, egg yolk and remaining sugar with a wooden spoon. Slowly pour the warm milk on to this, stirring all the time, then add the vanilla.

Butter the bread then layer it, buttered side up, in an ovenproof dish, sprinkling on the finely grated zest, raisins and Marsala as you go (if all the Marsala has been absorbed, sprinkle a little more on as you layer it). Pour the cream through a sieve on to the bread and leave to sit for 30 minutes (this just makes the pudding lighter). Preheat the oven to 180°C/350°F/gas mark 4.

Put the dish in a roasting tin and add enough boiling water to the tin to come halfway up the sides of the dish. Bake for 40–45 minutes, or until puffy, golden and set on the top (if you press the middle with your finger it should be *just* set). Leave to cool slightly, the pudding will continue to cook a little, then dust with icing sugar. Serve with crème fraîche or whipped cream.

raspberry yogurt cake

I HAD A LOVELY yogurt and raspberry cake in a café, The Field Kitchen, in Nettlebed near Henley, and could not get it out of my head. This is my version of the cake I couldn't forget. You do have to eat it on the day it's baked, otherwise the raspberries in the icing will spoil.

SERVES 10–12

For the cake
125g (4½oz) unsalted butter, plus more for the tin
225g (8oz) caster sugar
finely grated zest of 2 unwaxed lemons
½ tsp vanilla extract
2 large eggs, at room temperature, lightly beaten
300g (10½oz) plain flour, sifted
2 tsp baking powder

115g (4oz) natural yogurt
200g (7oz) raspberries

For the icing
150g (5½oz) icing sugar, sifted
2 tbsp lemon juice
about 10 raspberries

Preheat the oven to 180°C/350°F/gas mark 4. Butter a 22 x 12 x 7cm (8½ x 4½ x 2½in) loaf tin and line the base with baking parchment. Beat the butter and sugar until pale and fluffy, then add the lemon zest and vanilla. Add the eggs a little at a time, beating well after each addition. Put 2 tbsp of the flour in a bowl to toss with the raspberries later. Mix the remaining flour and baking powder together and fold this into the batter, alternating with spoonfuls of the yogurt.

Toss the raspberries with the reserved flour. Put one-third of the batter into the loaf tin and add half the raspberries, spreading them out evenly. Put another one-third of the batter on top, followed by the rest of the raspberries. Finish with the remaining batter.

Bake for one hour 15 minutes. A skewer inserted into the centre of the cake should come out clean. If the top seems to be colouring too much during cooking, cover it with foil. Leave the cake in the tin for 10 minutes, then turn it out on to a wire rack to cool.

Mix the icing sugar with the lemon juice until smooth. Spread about two-thirds of this on the cake. Partly crush the 10 raspberries and add them to the remaining icing. Don't completely mix them in, you just want them to stain bits of the icing. Pour over the cake. This won't set firmly, but do leave it to set a little before serving.

turkish mocha pots

MOST PUDDINGS IN TURKEY are fruit- or pastry-based, but I ate a spiced chocolate mousse when I was last there and decided to combine it with the flavours of a Turkish coffee. This is easy to make and there's no last-minute faffing about. Make sure you cover the pots with cling film, or they'll pick up other flavours while they're in the fridge.

SERVES 6

250ml (9fl oz) whole milk

250ml (9fl oz) double cream

ground seeds from 5 cardamom pods

½ cinnamon stick

4 tbsp soft dark brown sugar

2 tbsp cornflour

4½ tsp instant espresso coffee

200g (7oz) good-quality dark chocolate (70% cocoa solids), broken into pieces

25g (scant 1oz) unsalted butter

1 tsp vanilla extract

200ml (7fl oz) whipping cream

2 tbsp icing sugar, or to taste

chocolate-coated coffee beans

Put the milk and cream into a saucepan with the cardamom and cinnamon. Bring to the boil, then take off the heat and leave to sit for 30 minutes so the spices can flavour the milk. Strain.

Mix the sugar, cornflour and coffee together in a saucepan. Whisk in the milk mixture, adding it slowly so that no lumps form. Set over a medium heat and bring to the boil, stirring constantly, then take off the heat. Add the chocolate, butter and vanilla and whisk until the mixture is completely smooth and the chocolate has melted. Divide between six little pots or coffee cups. Cover with cling film and refrigerate for at least two hours to firm up.

Whip the cream, add the icing sugar and use it to decorate each pot or cup. Sprinkle with the chocolate-coated coffee beans to serve.

shopping guide

There is hardly an ingredient that you can't find online these days, but I recognize that no one wants to have to make an online order – with the delivery costs that entails – every week. I've tried to give alternatives for ingredients that are not easy to find (though supermarkets stock an incredible range of stuff these days), but there are a few you might need to track down. What I sometimes do is make a list of several ingredients and put in an order with a single company, to save money on delivery costs.

There are some grains used in this book that haven't quite made it into supermarkets yet (it's still hard to find farro, for instance, though you can substitute spelt) and also a few chilli pastes. My first stop is usually Souschef. They're quick, reliable and offer great customer service. For foods they don't have, try the other websites listed here, especially for unusual spices.

When it comes to harder-to-find fruit or vegetables, often markets, ethnic shops and small greengrocers are happy hunting grounds. Ocado now deliver everything that the fruit and veg importer Natoora sells (as well as their charcuterie and cheeses), so even esoteric items such as watermelon radishes (an optional extra in one of the dishes in this book) can be delivered right to your door.

I don't order fish online; I don't often buy it in supermarkets, either. I usually go to my fishmonger. I have a really good local butcher, too, but I buy the odd bit of meat from the supermarket. Never, however, pork. For that you do need a butcher and an excellent one at that. I don't like to be impractical or sound snobbish but, honestly, if my only option for pork chops is the supermarket, I just make something else instead. I also order some meat online, especially sausages, direct from the farm (Pipers are listed here, but there may be other amazing farms and farm shops in your area).

COOL CHILE CO
www.coolchile.co.uk

The best stockist for unusual dried chillies, especially South American varieties.

HEALTHY SUPPLIES
www.healthysupplies.co.uk

Not just for 'healthy' ingredients, but a particularly great source for pulses, wholegrains, seeds, nuts and dried fruits.

MELBURY AND APPLETON
www.melburyandappleton.co.uk

Ingredients listed by country. Great for grains and pulses.

PIPERS FARM
www.pipersfarm.com

An award-winning Devon-based company. Their sausages don't contain nitrates or nitrites, the preservatives used in most sausages that are linked with cancer (this means a short shelf life, so they send them out frozen). I can serve these without worrying. I don't overreact to health issues surrounding food – a little bit of everything is generally my motto – but if there's an issue raised with a food you eat often, it's sensible to bear it in mind.

SEASONED PIONEERS
www.seasonedpioneers.co.uk

For unusual spices; I've been using them for years.

SOUSCHEF
www.souschef.co.uk

Don't be put off by the name. They don't just cater for chefs. There's not much you can't find on this site.

THE ASIAN COOKSHOP
www.theasiancookshop.co.uk

A vast array, plus every pulse you've heard of (and some you haven't). Specialist Burmese, Caribbean, Chinese, Indian, Japanese, Mexican and Thai ingredients.

index

almonds: Andalusian chicken 220
  mint, almond & honey pesto 153
  rhubarb & raspberry crumble cake 299
  roast lamb loin fillets with zhoggiu 178
  summer fruit & almond cake 288
amaretti biscuits: apricot & amaretti crostata
  300
anchovies: anchovy & rosemary sauce 152
  linguine all'amalfitana 106
  mashed eggs with anchovy, shallots
    & parsley 67
  parsley-anchovy relish 194
  peperoni gratinati al forno 245
  pine nut & anchovy cream 152
  roast aubergines with crushed walnuts
    & anchovies 272
  roast lamb with peas, onions & vermouth 182
  salsa bianca 242
Andalusian chicken 220
apples: baked apples with marmalade
    & Southern Comfort cream 304
  baked sausages raisins & cider 206
  marmalade baked fruit with boozy orange
    cream 306
  roast apple & maple Eton mess 281
  roast apple, blackberry & whiskey trifles 304
apricots: apricot & amaretti crostata 300
  grilled apricots & honey 311
  roast apricot & orange blossom fool 282
artichokes, carrots & preserved lemons 256
asparagus: goat's cheese & warm butter 254
  fettuccine with asparagus, peas & saffron 101
aubergines: cumin-roast aubergines,
    chickpeas, walnuts & dates 74
  fragrant Sichuan aubergines 273
  Moroccan-spiced chicken with dates
    & aubergines 223
  roast aubergines with crushed walnuts
    & anchovies 272
  roast aubergines with tomatoes & saffron
    cream 274
avocados: cool greens, hot Asian dressing 37
  cumin-coriander roast carrots with
    pomegranates & avocado 31
  salad of chorizo, avocado & peppers 40
  salmon tartare & avocado on rye 68
  seared tuna with preserved lemon, olives
    & avocado 139
  spiced avocado with black beans, sour cream
    & cheese 65
  yogurt, avocado salsa & feta baked potato
    260

bacon: bacon & egg risotto 119
  bacon lardons, onions & Gruyère baked
    potato 260
  butternut strata 264
  warm salad of squid, bacon, beans
    & tarragon 46

baked beans, Greek 88
Balinese roast pork 174
bananas: roast banana & brown sugar fool 311
barley: smoked haddock, barley & spinach
    salad 116
beans see black beans; haricot beans etc
beetroot: food52 team salad 38
  roast beetroots with goat's cheese 265
  roast sweet & bitter vegetables 242
  spelt with blackberries, beets, walnuts
    & buttermilk 112
berries & melon in elderflower syrup 289
berries, meringues & curd cream 310
biberli cacık 266
black beans: spiced avocado with black beans,
    sour cream & cheese 65
black linguine with squid & spicy sausage 104
blackberries: blackberries & crème de cassis 311
  blackberry & caraway slaw 200
  roast apple, blackberry & whiskey trifles 304
  St Clements & rosemary posset with
    blackberries 309
  spelt with blackberries, beets, walnuts
    & buttermilk 112
blueberries: melon, blueberry & feta salad 45
borlotti beans: thyme-baked mushrooms &
    borlotti with roast garlic crème fraîche 86
bread: crostini with lardo & honey 50
  raisin, lemon & Marsala bread & butter
    pudding 324
  roast spatchcock with smoky migas 163
  see also toast
bream stuffed with walnuts & pomegranates
    130
Breton tuna & white bean gratin 78
brioche: toasted brioche with boozy
    mushrooms 62
broccoli with harissa & coriander gremolata
    239
bulgar wheat: lamb & bulgar pilaf 90
Burmese chicken 230
burrata with citrus, fennel & olives 48
butternut squash see squash

cakes: bitter flourless chocolate cake with
    coffee cream 318
  espresso loaf cake with burnt butter & coffee
    icing 322
  lemon & lavender cake 317
  lemon & ricotta cake 323
  raspberry yogurt cake 327
  rhubarb & raspberry crumble cake 299
  summer fruit & almond cake 288
canned food 84
carrots: artichokes, carrots & preserved lemons
    256
  carrot houmous 54
  cumin-coriander roast carrots with
    pomegranates & avocado 31

harissa roast carrots, white beans & dill 82
  roast sweet & bitter vegetables 242
  spelt with carrots & kale 118
Cashel Blue, walnuts & watercress baked
    potato 260
cauliflower: Parmesan roast chicken with
    cauliflower & thyme 228
  roast cauliflower with pomegranates, green
    olives & chickpea purée 89
  roast cauliflower with Spanish flavours 244
  roast sweet & bitter vegetables 242
cavolo nero, pappardelle with 94
chard: creamy gratin of rainbow chard & red
    chicory 248
cheese: bacon lardons, onions & Gruyère
    baked potato 260
  baked merguez with beans, eggs & feta 81
  biberli cacık 266
  burrata with citrus, fennel & olives 48
  butternut strata 264
  Cashel Blue, walnuts & watercress baked
    potato 260
  cider rarebit 60
  Greek baked beans 88
  greens with chilli, olive oil, eggs, feta
    & seeds 21
  griddled courgettes, burrata & fregola 26
  ham, Camembert & cream baked potato 261
  leek & feta omelette with sumac 22
  melon, blueberry & feta salad 45
  Mumbai toastie 57
  olive oil-braised leeks & peas with feta
    & dill 250
  oregano lamb chops with Greek htipiti 197
  orzo with lemon & parsley 100
  Parmesan roast chicken 228
  pasta all'ortolana 108
  peaches with burrata 50
  pistachio & feta pesto 153
  pork loin with pumpkin purée & pecorino 173
  Pugliese fish tiella 144
  roast squash with ricotta, smoked cheese
    & sage 236
  smoked haddock, Cheddar & spinach baked
    potato 261
  smoked haddock with a mature Cheddar
    crust 145
  spiced avocado with black beans, sour
    cream   & cheese 65
  spiced lamb cutlets with dates, feta, sumac
    & tahini 199
  Tim's Parmesan chicken 221
  tomatoes, soft herbs & feta 33
  yogurt, avocado salsa & feta baked potato
    260
  see also goat's cheese
chermoula 211
cherries: cucumber, radishes & cherries 28
  hot cherries with grappa & ice cream 294

acknowledgements

Part of what I do is collect recipes, from home cooks, friends and chefs. I did this before I started to write about food, and the exchange of dishes and ideas has been one of the great pleasures of my life. Roopa Gulati now has at least one recipe in every book I write (her food is just so good) and I thank her for the dishes in this volume (Mumbai toastie and Roopa's kheer with scented fruits). @foodwithmustard – who I met on Twitter and has become a friend – gave me the recipe for one of her family's favourite dishes, Ishita's masala chicken. Tim Bax is responsible for Tim's parmesan chicken; Sally Butcher, who owns the lovely Persian shop, Persepolis, in south London, allowed me to steal her Persian-inspired eggs; chef Ben Tish gave me the recipe for Roast cauliflower with Spanish flavours; the team at the American food website, Food52, served me the lovely apple, kohlrabi and beet salad (Food52 team salad) when I met them in New York last year; and Naomi Duguid gave me her knock-out recipe for Burmese chicken.

Huge thanks to my former and current editors at *The Telegraph* – Elfreda Pownall and Amy Bryant – for their support, their sifting of ideas, their dedication to the cause, and being a pleasure to work with. My publisher, Denise Bates, continues to 'get' it and creates an environment in which we can all do the best job possible. Also at Octopus I am grateful to Jonathan Christie, Katherine Hockley and Sybella Stephens for guiding this project through from manuscript stage to book. Dear Kevin Hawkins and Caroline Brown, you're just the best in the business.

Finally, the team: my editor, Lucy Bannell, designer Miranda Harvey, photographer, Laura Edwards and cooks Joss Herd and Rachel Wood. Thank you all for being inspiring, sparky, kind, fun, open-minded, patient, perfectionist and always going the extra mile. I appreciate all the work you do. The joy of collaborating with you means I am always writing a book (as I would miss you all too much if I wasn't). Particular thanks to Lucy, to whom this book is dedicated, for editing my words for 14 years (first at *The Telegraph* and then at my publishers) with the utmost care, and for unfailing friendship and support.